FACEBOOK ADVERTISING

TRENDS

— AND —

STRATEGIES

FOR E-COMMERCE
2019 EDITION

Printed in the USA
First Edition
ISBN: 978-0-6484407-0-3

Cover Design: Studio1 Design
Interior Design and Layout: Swish Design

To my fellow entrepreneurs, who pour every drop of energy into their businesses to achieve the life of their dreams.

CONTENTS

Introduction 1

Why Trends MATTER 2

The Anatomy of a Trend: A Play in Three Acts 3

Now, It's Your Turn! 7

CHAPTER 1 Amanda Bond: The Ad Strategist Speaks 9

2019 Facebook Ad Trends for E-Commerce Companies 10

What Companies Should be Doing to Adapt 10

What Companies Shouldn't be Doing in 2019 .11

Chatbots and the Brand Experience 12

Facebook Messenger Strategies to Adopt in 2019 13

Upcoming Trends in Facebook Advertising 14

Increasing Performance with Facebook Advertising in 2019 15

How to Evaluate the Effectiveness of Channels and Funnels for
Your Business 16

My Top Strategy to Generate Leads and Sales in 2019 17

Other Tips for E-Commerce Companies in 2019 19

CHAPTER 2 David Schloss: Social Advertising Specialist 21

Facebook Trends in 2019 22

What Companies Should Be Doing to Adapt 23

What Companies Should STOP Doing 24

An Example of Effective Video Strategy 25

Facebook Messenger and Chatbots. 26

Facebook's Future 29

Adapting to Facebook Trends to Increase Performance 30

My Top 3 Strategies for Generating E-Commerce Sales 32

CHAPTER 3 Enrico Lugnan: The Instagram Whisperer **37**

Tips for Leveraging Facebook and Instagram. 38

Identifying Influencers on Instagram. 40

Building Relationships with Influencers 40

Facebook Advertising Trends in 2019 41

What Companies Should Be Doing to Adapt 41

What Companies Shouldn't Be Doing in 2019 42

Facebook Messenger and Chatbots. 43

Facebook Advertising Throughout 2019 44

How Companies Can Maintain (or Even Increase)
Performance in 2019. 45

Strategies to Further Identify Customer Data. 45

Top 3 Strategies for E-Commerce Companies 46

Potential Longevity of These Tips and Strategies 47

CHAPTER 4 Janak Mehta: Facebook Ad Ninja **49**

2019 Trends in Facebook Advertising 50

Using Video Ads Effectively. 52

Chatbots and Messenger 53

Dynamic Product Ads 54

Current Facebook Ad Trends: What Not to Do 58

The (Near) Future of Messenger and Chatbots 59

Top 4 Strategies for E-Commerce Owners in 2019 and Beyond 60

Budgeting for Content Generation. 62

Possibility of Current Strategies Becoming Stale in the Near Future. . . .63

CHAPTER 5 Jeremy Howie: The Enlightened Marketing Expert **65**

Current Facebook Trends for E-Commerce Companies
Selling Products. 66

Making the Most of Facebook Live. 67

Future Facebook Trends. 68

Facebook Advertising "Don'ts" for E-Commerce Companies 68

Facebook Messenger 69

Future Developments in Facebook Advertising 71

Adapting to All These Changes and Maximizing ROI. 72

Top 3 Facebook Tips for E-Commerce. 72

Final Thoughts. 73

CHAPTER 6 Jeremy Wainwright: Growth Hacker **75**

Current Trends in Facebook Advertising: Differentiating
Yourself from the Competition in 2019 76

What E-Commerce Companies Need to Know in Order to
Really Build Their Business 77

Optimizing Strategy around the Recent Changes in Facebook 79

Facebook Messenger and Chatbots in 2019. .80

Facebook Advertising in the Near Future 81

Adapting, Maintaining and Increasing Performance in
E-Commerce Companies. 82

Top 3 Strategies for E-Commerce Companies in 2019 and Beyond 82

CHAPTER 7 Mari Connor: Business Strategist Extraordinaire **85**

Facebook Advertising Trends for E-Commerce in 2019 85

A Step-by-Step Guide to Creating This Facebook Advertising Funnel . .87

E-Commerce "Don'ts" for 2019. 88

Facebook Messenger and Chatbots in 2019. .89

Adapting and Maintaining/Increasing Performance in 2019 91

Other Trends Developing Going Into 2019. 93

Top 3 Strategies for 2019 93

CHAPTER 8 Mike Pisciotta: The Marketing Guru **97**

Facebook Advertising Trends of 2019 98

What Companies Can Do to Adapt to What's Happening in
Facebook...99

Why the Dizzying Array of Expanded Options for Advertisers?......100

How to Choose Among the New Options on Facebook 101

What E-Commerce Companies Should Start Doing in 2019 102

What E-Commerce Companies Should Stop Doing in 2019 104

Facebook Messenger and Chatbots in 2019.....................105

Facebook's Continuing Evolution Through The Year...............106

How to Improve Your Return on Ad Spend on Facebook
Advertising in 2019..107

Three Strategies to Use Throughout 2019 107

CHAPTER 9 Molly Pittman: The Consultant's Consultant **111**

Becoming a Successful Digital Marketer 112

Facebook Trends in 2019 113

The Importance of Branding 114

Why Some Companies Have So Much Trouble Telling a Story 115

What E-Commerce Companies Need to Do to Adapt in 2019.......116

What Companies Should STOP Doing in 2019 117

Current Trends in Facebook Messenger and Chatbots 120

The Future of Facebook Advertising.............................122

How E-Commerce Companies Can Keep Their Footing on the
Continuously Shifting Terrain....................................123

Three Strategies E-Commerce Companies Should Incorporate
Right Now...123

CHAPTER 10 Sam Bell: Social Ads Virtuoso...................... **125**

Adwords vs. Facebook 127

2019 Trends in Facebook Advertising for E-Commerce Companies...127

Facebook Essentials for E-Commerce Companies..................128

Facebook "Don'ts" for E-Commerce Companies 129

Choosing Your Products 129

Facebook Messenger and Chatbot "Don'ts". 130

Chatbot and Messenger "Don'ts". 131

Basic Rules for Using Segmentation 132

Facebook Advertising in 2019 132

Leveraging Audience Network Ads 133

Custom Event Conversions 134

Adapting, Maintaining, and Increasing Performance 135

Top 4 Strategies for E-Commerce Companies in 2019 136

CHAPTER 11 Trevor Chapman: The King of Disruptive
Digital Marketing **138**

Why Segment Now? 143

How to Create a More Effective Message 143

Dealing with Change 146

Creating Better Messaging 148

Messaging Mistakes Companies Make. 149

What Small Companies Should Stop Doing 151

The "Dos" and "Don'ts" of Facebook Messenger and Chatbots 151

The Future of Facebook 152

Three E-commerce Strategies to Implement Right Now 154

Strategies for Acquiring Leads with Facebook 157

The Shelf Life of Internet Marketing Strategy 158

Summary 159

CHAPTER 12 Rory Stern: The Compliance Artist **161**

Facebook Advertising Trends 162

How to Become the "Cream" 163

Mistakes to Avoid 164

What Companies Should Do to Adapt to Facebook's New
Developments 167

What Companies Shouldn't Do, Ever 170

Facebook Messenger and Chatbots 171

Facebook Advertising in 2019 173

Top 3 Strategies for E-Commerce Owners in 2019 174

CHAPTER 13 Josh Marsden: Ordinary Guy with

Extraordinary Vision **176**

Direct Response Marketing 181

Unique Direct Response Marketing 182

Successful Companies Still Have Room to Grow 182

Case Study: Texas Lone Star Tamales 183

2019 Trends in Facebook Ads 184

What E-Commerce Companies Should Be Doing to Adapt 186

What E-Commerce Companies Should *NOT* Be Doing in 2019 187

The Future of Facebook Advertising 188

Tips for Maintaining/Increasing Performance 189

Will These Tips and Strategies Continue to Work for the

Foreseeable Future? 190

Final Thoughts 191

The Good Stuff: The Top Tips, Strategies, and Tactics Featured

in the Book **193**

Amanda Bond 193

David Schloss 194

Enrico Lugnan 196

Janek Mehta 197

Jeremy Howie 199

Jeremy Wainwright 200

Mari Connor 201

Mike Pisciotta 202

Molly Pittman 203

Sam Bell 204

Trevor Chapman 206

Rory Stern. 208

Josh Marsden 210

Conclusion **213**

Acknowledgements **217**

Stay in touch **221**

FACEBOOK

ADVERTISING

TRENDS

— AND —

STRATEGIES

FOR E-COMMERCE

2019 EDITION

JOSH MARSDEN, MBA

INTRODUCTION

As entrepreneurs, we experience great peaks and deep valleys, often struggling to keep our dreams in sight. However, no matter what life throws at us, we overcome every obstacle, often through sheer determination. This is what makes us great – our warrior spirit and our willingness to tackle the toughest challenges of entrepreneurship while maintaining a can-do attitude and a positive mindset. Some are better at it than others, but when push comes to shove, we all roll up our sleeves and find a way to soldier through. You have it. I have it. It's what makes us the leaders we are in today's world, and it's how and why we succeed.

This book is written for the e-commerce owners who are passionate about growing their businesses, and are always seeking to stay ahead of the curve with Facebook Advertising. The ones who refuse to stop until they achieve their goals, whether that goal is driven by a desire to provide value to others, create a better life for themselves, or improve the lives of those around them. If you're one of these remarkable people, this book is for you.

This book is also for the successful, thriving business owner who may or may not be using Facebook Advertising effectively and profitably – going through this book will help you avoid making costly errors while you're figuring out how to take advantage of the current trends in Facebook Advertising.

In this book, you'll learn from some of the best of the best in the Facebook Advertising industry today. It contains wisdom and advice from 12 Facebook Advertising specialists – their take on what trends are causing the biggest ripples, and suggestions on how to use Facebook Advertising effectively. Their input is vital and relevant, and is what makes this book such a powerful tool for helping you achieve your Facebook Advertising goals in 2019. Hats off to Jeremy Howie, Amanda Bond, Rory Stern, Jeremy Wainwright, Janak Mehta, Mike Pisciotta, Molly Pittman, Enrico Lugnan, Sam Bell, David Schloss, Mari Connor, and Trevor Chapman for their invaluable contributions to the book. These luminaries in the field have graciously agreed to share some of their most powerful, "trend-resistant" strategies, which have been tested over and over again with great results. When you read this book, you'll get practical advice and strategies that you can implement right away in your own business, as well as a deeper understanding of Facebook's profound influence on advertising in today's climate.

As the main author behind the book, I'll also throw in my own two cents about Facebook Advertising trends going into 2019. I'll share several Facebook Advertising and Marketing Funnel strategies that can directly impact your lead generation and sales performance in your business in the weeks and months ahead.

WHY TRENDS MATTER

The forward-thinking men and women who are able to spot trends, adapt, and boldly seize opportunities are consistently the victors in any business competition.

However, many people find themselves stuck, afraid to change. As humans, we fear the unknown, and when paradigms shift, the resulting new trends can cause big ripples. We can either cling to our comfort zone and ignore them, give in to the fear, or take a deep breath and embrace the change.

Ignoring trends is tempting – given the choice, most people would elect to freeze time so everything could remain familiar and comfortable. But when you are a business owner, ignoring trends can lead to a whole host of undesirable outcomes. Your competitors who decide to "ride" the trend are bound to experience growth, potentially leaving you and your business in the dust.

In addition, market trends affect platforms like Facebook, which can respond by changing policies that can cause your ads to be shut down and your account to be disabled in a heartbeat, leading you to lose your vital lead generation source. If you're aware of shifting trends, however, you can give yourself the time you need to adapt your strategy in order to avoid this outcome; if you're studiously ignoring trends, you leave your company vulnerable to this kind of damage.

Fear in a business setting, on the other hand, typically leads to inaction. Fear will keep you from pursuing opportunities that could change the course of your life and your business. It will keep you stuck in place, and it will keep you from succeeding. Inaction only leads to blind comfort, and as we all know, you can never be comfortable in business!

Over the next several pages, Henry Ford, Elon Musk, the Winklevoss Twins, and several others will demonstrate how following trends can be smart, powerful, and lucrative.

This book will show you how to get past your fear of change and help you adapt to the changes happening in Facebook Advertising for 2019.

Then, you'll learn from some of the best Facebook advertisers on the planet! The 12 other Facebook Advertising specialists that have contributed to this book and I will help you understand what's happening in the field right now, what's coming soon, and what thoroughly-tested strategies will continue to work, regardless of the trends that take place in Facebook.

Go ahead and dive in…

THE ANATOMY OF A TREND: A PLAY IN THREE ACTS

The Model T Trend in the Automobile Industry

Let's start by rewinding the clock back to 1908, when a lifelong engine enthusiast named Henry Ford noticed a hot new trend in transportation…

Over the previous decades, automobiles had gradually been making their way into the public eye all over the world. The introduction of steam-powered boats and railroads in the early 1800s captured the public's interest. After that, it was inevitable that personal transportation would also start to evolve from the horse-powered buggies and stagecoaches of the previous era towards something faster and more self-powered.

The first automobile was built by French inventor Nicolas Joseph Cugnot in 1769. It didn't look much like the cars we know today – it was basically a stripped-down wheeled cart (he called it a "steam dray") with a single seat, no walls or roof, and a huge steam engine attached to the front. At the time, it was considered an interesting experiment, but ultimately deemed an impractical failure due to its inconvenient setup, noisiness, and high production cost. It was also unreliable, the controls tended to "freeze up," and the steam engine needed constant relighting, resulting in a conveyance that stalled regularly. Eventually, the cumbersome design, difficult maneuverability, unreliable power, and expensive manufacture led to the project being abandoned, and steam-engine-based automobiles were deemed a kind of noble washout.

But, while Cugnot's own project may have been unsuccessful, its legacy lived on – the idea of a self-powered personal transportation machine sparked the imagination of other inventors, who tested out alternative methods of creating an automobile. Scottish inventor Robert Anderson developed the first electric vehicle (that's right, Elon Musk didn't come up with this particular idea), then American Thomas Davenport made a more practical version. Meanwhile, two more French inventors, Gaston Planté and Camille Faure, invented the rechargeable lead-acid storage battery that was used in some of these early electric cars. Even Thomas Edison had a hand in this field, improving the electric batteries that powered the earliest "general use" electric cars. However, even with all of these advances, it just wasn't quite enough. No matter the improvements, the batteries maintained some basic characteristics that made them extremely inconvenient, even in the early 1900s. The charge didn't last long enough, limiting travel range to an average of 20-35 miles. As a result, the battery-powered automobile never emerged as the standard for modern transportation.

Then, a breakthrough. In 1886, Karl Benz was awarded a patent for the first gas-powered automobile. This was a huge development, the next big step in the quest to make automobiles a viable consumer good. Gas-powered automobiles had none of the downsides of the battery-powered version – at the time, the "material" they ran on was plentiful, the engines themselves were reliable, and they were able to travel longer distances without the need to refill (and, when necessary, the refilling process took significantly less time). This made the vehicle easier to handle. However, ultimately, it wasn't Karl Benz that brought gas-powered automobiles to the masses…

It was Henry Ford with the Model T.

Ford foresaw the massive potential of this new breed of personal transportation vehicle, and made the single biggest contribution that allowed the automobile to become a staple of modern living – he invented a streamlined assembly line process for mass producing these new gas-powered machines, cutting the manufacturing time of a single unit from 12 hours to 2.5 hours. This decreased production costs to the point where they could be priced for the average consumer.

This did the trick, and by 1918, nearly half of all automobiles owned by Americas were Model Ts.

This is why adapting to trends is so vital for any business. Henry Ford spotted an emerging trend, saw its potential, and found a way to adapt his efforts to capitalize on it. Just by doing this one thing, Henry Ford turned himself into a titan of industry, his name still synonymous with automobiles even now, over 100 years later.

Trends evolve, but the need to stay ahead of them is one of those underlying business concepts that never change. If you're a marketer or business owner, you need to keep a close eye on emerging trends, and have a quickly implementable plan in place to capitalize on them with Facebook Advertising.

The Zip2 Trend that Launched Elon Musk

From our vantage point in 2018, it seems insane, but when it first came into being, the internet was actually considered a fad! Unbelievable, right?

The idea that eventually became the internet was conceived by an MIT scientist, J.C.R. Licklider, in the early 1960s as a means to connect computer networks. Over the next 20 years, several iterations of this original idea were created. Eventually, these designs became ARPANET (designed to protect vulnerable lines of communication from the Russians during the Cold War) in the 1980s. Within a decade, ARPANET morphed into the World Wide Web, a global information network that was an early version of the internet we know today.

When the internet was first widely opened to the public in the early '90s, two brothers, Kimbal and Elon Musk, grasped the potential possibilities in this newly emerging trend. They developed online "city guides"-type software, which allowed a user to look up information about local businesses, get directions, and communicate with the businesses without having to call them.

This was still a fairly new concept at the time, with no guarantee of success. But the Musk brothers believed in their vision, and after securing funding from angel investors, left their comfort zone in Canada, moved to Palo Alto, and launched their company, Zip2.

While in Palo Alto, the Musks did whatever they had to do in order to bring their vision to life. In an effort to keep their costs in check, they ate only cheap fast food and slept in their office, spending every waking moment developing their business.

Eventually, they decided to focus on leasing their software to newspapers around the country, giving the newspapers an online presence while providing their subscribers with electronic directories, calendars, etc. – basically a more interactive way to plan their local activities.

The Musks' perseverance paid off – they grew Zip2 into a very successful early internet business. Within 3 years, Zip2 had over 160 national newspapers using their service. A year later, Compaq purchased Zip2 for $307 million, which was the first stepping-stone to Elon Musk becoming the global icon he is today.

In other words, the Musk brothers saw a trend, quickly figured out how to capitalize on its potential, and went for it with everything they had – the rest is history.

The Cryptocurrency Revolution

These days, you can hardly go 5 minutes without hearing a breathless news story about one cryptocurrency or another. However, back in 2009 when the first of them, Bitcoin, was launched, most people hadn't even heard of cryptocurrency, let alone knew anything about it. Bitcoin emerged with little fanfare, and with the majority of the world tuning it out, disregarding it, and/ or seeing it as nothing but "hype."

But a few sharp-eyed trend spotters took notice…

One was Jared Kenna, who invested $1,000 into Bitcoin when it first emerged. This came right on the heels of the catastrophic 2008 stock market crash in the United States. At the time, bitcoins were only twenty cents a coin. That's right, if you can believe it – twenty cents. Although he didn't know much about Bitcoin, Jared decided that, given the state of the market, his best bet would be to keep his investing outside of the typical, increasingly unreliable, mainstream currencies. Today, that initial $1,000 investment is worth almost $30 million…

Then there are the Winklevoss twins, another early Bitcoin success story. If the name sounds familiar, even though you don't generally keep tabs on the cryptocurrency market, you may recognize it from their famous lawsuit against Mark Zuckerberg (or from the movie, The Social Network).

Cameron and Tyler Winklevoss first came into the public eye in 2004, when they sued Mark Zuckerberg, claiming he had stolen the idea for Facebook from them. After a lengthy court case, the Winklevosses received a $65 million settlement. They invested $11 million of that settlement into Bitcoin in 2013. That initial investment is now worth $1.3 billion.

Another Bitcoin success story involves a guy who did the equivalent of shoving his Bitcoin investment in a back pocket, and forgetting all about it until laundry day. In 2009, after stumbling onto Bitcoin while researching encryption for a thesis, Norwegian graduate student Kristoffer Koch purchased $26.60 worth of bitcoins (5,000 bitcoins at the time). Then, he promptly forgot all about it. It wasn't until 2013, when the buzz surrounding Bitcoin led to a flurry of news reports, that he suddenly remembered that he had invested in the currency early on. He checked his online ledger to see how much his small investment was now worth. Much to his delight, he found that the $26.60 he spent in 2009 had turned into $886,000 in 2013. That's one crazy return in a short span of 4 years!

NOW, IT'S YOUR TURN!

Jared, Cameron, Tyler, and Kristoffer are all prime examples of how the ability to recognize trends and adapt to them can lead to incredible profits.

Facebook advertising is the same. If you make a concerted effort to stay on top of the changes happening in Facebook advertising and quickly adapting your company's strategy to these changes, you have the potential to do amazing things for your business's bottom line.

It may sound daunting, but honestly, there's nothing to worry about – no matter what changes take place, there is **always** a way to adapt. It really just comes down to taking 100% ownership whenever a change occurs. Just by reading this book, you're taking the first step towards being able to confidently and successfully negotiate any Facebook advertising challenges head-on, regardless of what's happening with the platform.

Over the next several chapters, you'll hear from the Facebook Advertising specialists that we've assembled for the book. I encourage you to read them carefully, so that you too can profit wildly by leveraging the new Facebook Advertising trends for 2019.

CHAPTER 1

Amanda Bond: The Ad Strategist Speaks

I'm Amanda Bond, owner of The Ad Strategist, where we help people stop guessing and start getting results with their Facebook ads.

Speaking of which, have you noticed how the entire Facebook advertiser community seemed to have lost its collective mind when the recent updates to the algorithm were announced? Crazy, right? From the generalized panic, you'd think that this was the first time this sort of change was announced. But, of course, that's not exactly the case – Facebook algorithm updates actually happen a lot! And honestly, just like with previous updates, there's really nothing to fear here.

This purpose of this algorithm change was basically just to re-prioritize community and connection on the platform. It only became a whole ordeal because a lot of brands did quite a bit of fear mongering about it. They made it seem like this change signaled the end of Facebook as we know it. Now, full disclosure – I might have taken part in a little bit of that click-baitiness in my headlines and titles too. For example, I used the headline, "Is this the end of your Facebook page?" when I did a Facebook Live, but that's only because this was the type of thing that people were clicking right then.

It was just my headlines, though – all of the information in my actual pages actually said, "Listen, it's time to double down on your Facebook page, because now engagement is retargetable with our Facebook ads, and we can grow our warm audience from this. Also, Facebook is prioritizing it, so you'll get in front of more people with the updates." I actually think the changes are brilliant. I did take advantage of the fear mongering to get people to click, but only so I could tell them that this algorithm change is actually the best thing ever![1]

2019 FACEBOOK AD TRENDS FOR E-COMMERCE COMPANIES

One of the biggest recent trends is the need for dynamic sequences. If you have an e-commerce company, you can't just rely on cold traffic (i.e. sending people to the sales page and crossing your fingers, hoping that they transact right then and there) anymore. The brands that are going to win are those that take the time to curate a customer journey after that customer lands on their site. It's about creating a customer experience, and addressing the things that are keeping the customers from buying in the first place.

Maybe they need to see more use cases. Maybe they need to understand how the product works, or the benefits of it. Your job is to figure out what's stopping the customers from buying, and then using that in retargeting. The solution, by the way, isn't always a price discount. In fact, in my opinion, it's rarely the answer – with our clients, we don't discount the product to get them to take action most of the time; we simply show that product in different use cases.

WHAT COMPANIES SHOULD BE DOING TO ADAPT

There are three buckets that we call "Connect," "Commit," and "Convert." These correlate to awareness, conversion, and monetization. In order to adapt, you essentially need to take a step back and think about your sales process in those three phases.

How are you going to position your brand? That's the long-term vision and the growth that you're going to experience overall, if you can nail the branding aspect.

---

[1] Side note: I actually have a great book or recommendation to go along with this concept. If you're looking to understand the psychology of consumers and/or a little bit more about how the media works, pick up Ryan Holiday's, "Trust Me, I'm Lying." Fascinating stuff.

Then, how are you going to convert people? How are you going to get them to your sales pages, how are you going to get them onto your retargeting lists, your website, your email lists, things of that nature?

And then, what do they need to hear to actually make an educated purchase decision?

Because of all the noise being generated by the millions of advertisers who are now active on the platform, we need to become more judicious when guiding our audience to a purchase consideration. It's no longer enough to simply create an ad and expect potential customers to think, "Well, I've never seen this in my timeline before, so I'm going to buy it!" People are a lot savvier about the process now, and they also want to be wooed a little. We need to remember that, and start our sales transactions in a different way – not going straight in for the kill, but instead really starting to build a relationship with our audience.

WHAT COMPANIES SHOULDN'T BE DOING IN 2019

The first thing is the simplest thing – don't be a Spammy McSpammerson! In other words, don't just hammer the features of a product. Having ads that basically scream, "Feature-feature-feature-feature!" and/or "It's got all the features, and is this much off! Now, it's that much off!" becomes spammy-feeling really quickly.

It's a much better idea to be more personable with your brands, and give people a better experience. If you're not thinking about the brand experience that you're providing to people, you're leaving a lot of money on the table – you're not giving them a chance to transact on the front end, because they think, "Ew, you're gross, don't talk to me." Which means you're also not taking advantage of things like LTV (lifetime value), where people want to come back and transact with your brand again because you've given them a great customer experience. That's important too, because as we know, when you make more money from customers, you can spend more money on advertising along the way, and have some more fun with it too.

Love Saranghae, a Korean skincare company, is a perfect example of an entity that provides a fantastic brand experience. Normally, when you think of skincare, you think of advertisement in the style of L'Oréal or Maybelline or one of the other big beauty brands. However, Love Saranghae doesn't make glossy ads; instead, they do these kind of experiential trials on Instagram. I really like watching the way that they're dynamically using their stories to position their products, feature their community, and showcase people actually using their products in order to attract new customers. They're an e-comm brand that takes its digital strategy very seriously, but in a really fun way. It's an attitude worth mirroring. Check them out!

CHATBOTS AND THE BRAND EXPERIENCE

I'm on the fence about chatbots. I think that, used correctly, they can be beneficial. However, I've also seen them used extremely poorly, where the exchange feels so automated that it's obvious you're speaking to software. We all know that companies use bots – we understand that – but when it's set up badly, the whole interaction can feel unpleasantly disconnected.

I've used them in a previous launch of my program – we sent all of our sales conversations to a chatbot essentially to kick things off; from there, the users were directed over to a human experience. I think that's the most successful application – using chatbots to augment the brand experience, and to help people resolve basic inquiries. They can be great for answering frequently asked questions, or guiding people to the items they're looking for. As long as it's kept relatively simple, a bot can be a good additional resource. Just avoid trying to use them for functions they can't easily handle, to the point where it's actually detrimental to people's experience as they realize that, for all points and purposes, they're speaking to a computer.

The best way to seamlessly incorporate a chatbot is to actually go through the chat history on your page (or in your personal pages, if you talk about business there), and pull the conversations you've had. I think this is the root of my biggest hesitation about using bots more often – I just haven't taken the time to go through and build out something that has those natural language patterns[2] in my own business.

---

[2] *I love this expression – thank you, Scott Oldford!*

FACEBOOK MESSENGER STRATEGIES TO ADOPT IN 2019

The first step is to figure out where you would want to use Facebook Messenger and chatbots in a sequence, and why. I know it's tempting to just dive in headfirst, but that can actually muddy up your potential customers' journey. I would take a step back and map out the entire funnel, the intentions at each stage, and really ask, "Is this going to augment the experience? Is this going to create the access that people are looking for at each transition point?"

If the answer is no, that's okay – we don't always have to add another tool to make the conversions better. You can choose where (or if) to add new components. Let's use webinar attendance rates as an example: let's say you have a webinar, and you notice that attendance rates are dropping, but everything else in the funnel is strong. Your goal is to increase these rates, because obviously, more people convert when they attend live. So you might decide to use a chatbot at that one point in the funnel, and that's enough for now. In other words, get really clear on where bots can augment the funnel, but don't do it just for the sake of doing it.

That said, incorporating Messenger can have a huge impact on the overall success of marketing efforts. For instance, we had a client who was spending approximately $18 per person to get attendees for a webinar they were hosting. It worked out to something like $4 per lead, with show-up rates somewhere in the neighborhood of 20% to 25% (they were in a very crowded niche). So at the end of the day, we were spending $18 to get somebody to attend the webinar live. We then simulcast the same webinar on Facebook, and then amplified the content over on Facebook and tracked the results of the two.

When comparing the entire process of the webinar (taking people through the journey of landing on the registration page, waiting maybe three days before they attend the webinar, and then actually attending) vs. Facebook (showing it to them when they're live in that experience), Facebook won hands-down. They both converted at the same levels, but it ended up costing approximately 5 to 7 times less to get somebody to watch 95% of the Facebook Live video than to actually take them off the platform on the business's timeline, because it was just easier for them.

There's so much scaling potential, and so many opportunities to create some incredible dynamic sequences from that. For example, let's say you do a webinar on Facebook Live and get as many people as you can to watch it live, but then you amplify it afterwards and create different pathways based on their actions.

Somebody watched three seconds? Just keep serving them bits of video until they watch more.

Somebody hit 25%? Maybe that's enough to start seeding the actual original offer.

And then, let's say somebody hit 95% – they're highly motivated, so maybe we can go straight to the sale from there.

So if we reach out to them on Facebook (again, the platform that the audience is already *on*), we can create dynamic audiences off the back end without interrupting their experience.

UPCOMING TRENDS IN FACEBOOK ADVERTISING

The first trend I expect – and this is going to sound strange, especially for beginner audiences – is that interest targeting is going to be less important overall, primarily due to the increased intelligence levels of options like lookalikes. The AI is starting to be able to predict behavior better, casting a wide net and locating people who are likely to take actions based on other, similar people who are taking similar action.

The algorithm behind that part of the system is getting incredibly powerful, and as it continues to improve, it will become better at finding the people who are the most likely to take the actions that you want them to take. As this occurs, things like targeting very specific niche audiences of people based on the pages they've curated will become less important.

As a result, we're going to see advanced marketers focus less and less on these more traditional targeting strategies (those that aren't already doubling down on lookalikes alone, that is).

Another trend is an increased focus on videos, because it is a format that converts. Facebook just reported in this update that the live video format is **six times** more engaging than regular video. So we're going to be seeing a lot more brands adding videos into their customer journey – whether by creating a regular weekly live show or launch-based live-streaming, or in some other, not-yet-imagined way – in the near future.

Also, I anticipate more people using sequences, creating them around questions like: What do people need in order to make a decision? How do we get them there? How do we guide people towards making decisions and becoming more educated purchasers?

Another thing that I'm seeing a lot of people doing is simplifying their strategies, and often their overall business plans. There was a while there when things got really chaotic in terms of how funnels were put together and presented, and I think this new trend is a reaction to that. I've noticed that a lot of the people that I network with in this industry, a lot of clients and colleagues, are really streamlining their offers – honing in on the magic part of their business and getting rid of everything else.

INCREASING PERFORMANCE WITH FACEBOOK ADVERTISING IN 2019

The key to this is actually another trend that I haven't mentioned yet – for a lot of people, this is going to be The Year of Diversification. I believe advertisers are going to start looking around and investigating their options, instead of being so single-platform (e.g. Facebook) reliant.

Take, for example, a company I know that has 75% - 95% of their traffic from paid media through Facebook. What would they do if something were to happen to Facebook? Their entire multi-million dollar business could come crashing down. It's too risky to bet all of that on one platform.

I've been hearing a lot of talk about expanding horizons and testing other platforms once people have one mastered. That's an important point – this isn't a tip for anyone who's just getting started with Facebook advertising; this is for people who have their funnels and their conversions dialed in, and they're ready to take it to the next level. It's all about identifying what the next important platform could be for your company, really getting into that testing, and then getting out there. This doesn't always have to be a paid strategy; it could be influencer marketing or even just old-school doubling down on SEO for your blog.

The people who are going to win in 2019 are those who are taking a little bit of control back, building businesses that aren't so reliant on Facebook. Diversification is a great way to be able to adapt to a changing environment, and to weather any storms that might throw any single traffic channel's performance off.

HOW TO EVALUATE THE EFFECTIVENESS OF CHANNELS AND FUNNELS FOR YOUR BUSINESS

This is actually one of the major challenges of Facebook. It can be difficult to figure out which attributes are working, and what the full impact of your combined marketing efforts is. How does this attribution look across multiple platforms? How do we know that this effort was stacked on top of that effort, which led to this effort over here, and then transacted as a sale over here? It is really hard to pinpoint. However, if you can add any elements of attribution, if you can add UTM tags, if you can add sources to things that you do, that helps immensely – the more data that you have to work with, the better off you're going to be.

Start by asking yourself where you are in your business. If you're just getting started, maybe you don't need to know every single effect of every single social media post that you put out there. On the other hand, if you're a 7- or 8-figure business, knowing those things makes a big difference in being able to maximize the ROI of your advertising efforts.

This is another area where that idea of simplification comes into play: the more complexity there is to your business, the harder it is to track the results of all your combined and/or cross-platform efforts.

One of the most important things you can do to help yourself with this is to be almost compulsively organized on the back end. A real-life example I experienced today: we're preparing for an upcoming launch of a digital program for one of our clients. Today, we discovered that there were some pixel-tracking issues somewhere in the landing pages. A team of 25 people had put these landing pages together. However, it turned out that no one had ever archived anything in the system, so going back through the landing pages to try and find the error was an absolute nightmare. We ended up digging through years of information, none of which was aggregated or organized or even clearly labeled. The data was pure chaos, and I spent the day trying very hard not to bang my head against the table. The moral of this story is, as your business evolves, and/or you pivot towards new products or offers, take the time to archive the old stuff, create new systems, and track those new systems all the way through.

MY TOP STRATEGY TO GENERATE LEADS AND SALES IN 2019

The biggest strategy that we're deploying right now is growing our custom audiences as the first touch point. So instead of going straight for lead generation or straight for a sale, we're slowing down a bit and creating a few purposeful touch points before asking for those things. For example, I just set up a sequence – there's that word again! – where the audience will watch an indoctrination video, and even if they only watch three seconds, it's still a brand touch point. Then they'll be shown a series of lead magnets that they can opt into to move into the funnel. Instead of just going straight to cold traffic, we're taking that minute to really familiarize people with the brand and find ways to keep the brand at the forefront of their minds, because we understand that somebody can circle around the brand for, say, three months before they make a purchase. We try to shorten that timeline as much as possible by doing whatever we can to stay top-of-mind and relevant to our audience, delivering content to help them make a purchase decision.

I'm a big believer in employing content-first strategies. Whenever I speak to anyone (including clients) about this topic, I make a point of explaining the big-picture benefits, explaining how a content-first strategy and how creating those dynamic sequences will actually lower their CPA in the long run.

Of course, like with anything else, the process can have highs and lows. It's like when you first start a weight-loss regimen. You start doing all the right things, eating all the right foods and drinking all the water. Then all of a sudden, you start to feel bloated, and you're like, "What is actually happening? I'm doing all these good things for my body – why am I bloated?" Well, it's all that water weight. Your body is making the changes necessary to become more efficient, and that transition might be uncomfortable, and yes, you might feel bloated for a minute during the adjustment.

The first month of implementing a content-first strategy is like that too. At first, you're just trying to find out what works and what converts. There's going to be a lot of bloat and a lot of waste that happens during that time, and you have to mentally prepare for the extra dollars going out the door in order to get the data that you need. But once you find the efficiencies, it's like you shed all that water weight, and all of a sudden your newfound muscles start to show.

Even the efforts that don't end up working provide you with more data to look at, so you don't want to restrict yourself to just one ad where all you have is your cost per lead to go off of. You're going to want to make sure that you're competing as hard as you can on all the different split tests that you're doing, because an increase of just a few percentage points to the conversion of your cold audience is going to make a massive difference to your lead generation.

When you're putting together sequences you're able to see the big picture, to figure out, "Okay, this one's a little bit lower over here, so maybe I'll just swap in some different content." So in the grand scheme of things, you're actually building massive momentum with all the data, versus confining yourself to finding these small, incremental pieces in an effort to save money on leads. You need to look at earnings per lead for the revenue, or the ROAS (return on ad spend) side of the equation. As in that larger strategy, all these little tweaks are adding up to an increased ROAS along the way.

For anyone who's skeptical about spending money to promote content-first, keep in mind that you pay one of two ways: either with money or with time. Are you willing to spend your money to get that data faster so that you can iterate faster so you can get results faster? Or are you willing to spend your time or your employees' time to do the exact same thing through hustle and hard work? You make the decision: one's fast; the other's a lot of effort. That's it.

Part of that decision has to do with where you are in your business. Sometimes cash flow isn't at a place where you can test with your money, so you have to test with your time, and vice versa. That's just how it goes.

OTHER TIPS FOR E-COMMERCE COMPANIES IN 2019

The biggest strategy that I advocate is: stop trying to funnel-hack everyone else's everything, and be true to your own brand values. Figure out what your brand's about, how your brand sells, how you connect with your customers, and double down on what's working. One of the biggest changes that we made in my own business was to stop duplicating the efforts of others, and just go with what we intuitively know our audience wants. Now, I say "intuitively," but that intuition is based on data that has previously supported it. So really, go with what the data shows your audience wants, and build a funnel based around that – don't build a funnel just because Joe Blow from some other e-comm company is doing it!

If that means revisiting a strategy that has worked for your company in the past but isn't "trendy" now, go for it. Even though I've been talking a lot about visioning forward and the customer journey, there is still a place where you can go straight-to-sale for some companies, there is still a place where cold-traffic-to-leads can still work. Every business is unique, and if a tried-and-tested campaign has worked in the past, it's very likely that under the right circumstances, it's going to work again. In my company, for example, while we're focused on dynamic sequences, we're also still deploying lead campaigns constantly, and testing and re-iterating. We haven't abandoned the strategies that worked for us in the past – it's just that these lead campaigns have taken on a different role within the bigger picture of what we do with clients or what we do in our own businesses.

I think the biggest takeaway from all of this is that, at the end of the day, all of your results are just ones and zeros. They're just bits of data that let you see what works and what doesn't, allowing you to adjust your approach accordingly. When you're an entrepreneur, you live and breathe for your business, and it's easy to take things personally and get caught up in the drama of that. But I've always found that, when we take our emotions out of the equation and just look at a situation for what it is, it creates the space we need to find better solutions along the way.

Do you want to see how we have a 1500+ Return on Adspend in a competitive E-Commerce market? You can learn how to get back $15 for every $1 spend on Facebook Ads by going to **www.cvoaccel.com/success.**

CHAPTER 2

David Schloss: Social Advertising Specialist

I'm David Schloss, and I help influencers, celebrities, personal brands, and companies of all sizes to grow their social presence. Although there are many ways that this can be accomplished, my company's focus is primarily on Facebook and Instagram advertising, with some YouTube ads thrown in here and there.

It all started in my college apartment back in 2007. At the time, I was just trying to figure out how to make money online. A random little Google search on this topic led me down a gigantic rabbit hole of tactics and strategies, SEO, video marketing, etc. I spent a couple of years dabbling in various pursuits within the field – basically, anything that seemed like it might be interesting – but found that most of them simply took too long to deliver results. I didn't want people to have to wait 3 or 4 months before they saw progress.

I kept searching, and eventually stumbled across social advertising. Once I did, it just clicked – I had finally found something that I felt absolutely passionate about, and which provided almost immediate results.

After a lot of trial and error, I eventually settled on a combination of platforms that works really well for my company and its customers. We started using Facebook and Instagram when they first opened up their respective ad spaces to the public (approximately 9 years ago for Facebook; 3 years ago for Instagram). Our results have been pretty spectacular. Not only does the narrow focus on only 2 platforms keeps us from getting spread too thin, the combination of Facebook and Instagram just *works*!

FACEBOOK TRENDS IN 2019

Facebook recently went through a whole host of algorithmic changes. Certain types of content that were previously allowed are now banned, and vice versa.

For example, throughout most of Facebook's history, ads for dating sites were forbidden. However, during the most recent series of site changes, the restrictions on this content were loosened. Now, we're starting to see a lot more advertising from matchmakers and dating specialists – professionals who are in the business of helping others to find their ideal matches.

On the other hand, advertising for cryptocurrencies and ICOs (initial coin offering) – so hot in 2017 and very early 2018 – are now prohibited.

This isn't new, or even unexpected. Since it opened its ad platform, Facebook has done this sort of "clean sweep" periodically. Once or twice a year, a massive ban hammer occurs: accounts get shut down, new categories of ads come flooding in, and CPMs (cost per 1,000 ad impressions) and CPCs (cost per click) skyrocket. It's all temporary, of course, but the changes typically cause mass hysteria: advertisers lose their minds, Facebook's stock goes crazy because the stockholders don't know what's going on, etc. But this is just part of their process, of their ongoing effort to clean up the network.

Obviously, Facebook has a vested interest in ensuring its longevity. In pursuit of that, they try to create a News Feed that's both relevant and valuable to their users. Yes, ostensibly, Facebook's main purpose is to provide a platform where you can communicate with friends, family, colleagues, clients, etc. – everyone in your life. But it's also there to connect you with the world at large, so Facebook takes pains to make sure that the ads in that News Feed (and your groups and your Messenger) are content that you actually want to see. So if you're actively engaging with something online – products for gaming, or for your business, or whatever it may be – they ensure that those products actually appear in your feed because you've already demonstrated an interest in them.

This, of course, is the ideal scenario. In real life, however, more often than not, the ads that target individuals are random. Users are often targeted with ads that have absolutely nothing to do with them. People regularly post screenshots of random ads they receive, along with comments like, "I don't know why I'm seeing this." It's like when I occasionally have an ad for AARP pop up in my feed. I'm 29 years old – that just doesn't make any sense! I'm clearly not who they meant to target.

So when Facebook changes its algorithms, what it's trying to do is make sure the ads that individual users see are for things that they would actually engage with; things that they want to interact with, and to like, and to comment on, and to share. Otherwise, not only are they not serving their subscribers; they're running the risk of losing users' attention altogether. If people start to see the ads as an annoyance, they'll hide them or ignore them, and Facebook becomes a much less attractive prospect for advertising dollars. Plus, if the users get irritated enough, they might just leave Facebook.

Obviously, these are outcomes that Facebook wants to avoid at all costs. The last thing they want is to become another MySpace, a giant platform that suddenly has a mass user exodus to some other app. So Facebook continuously improves its algorithm, making sure that, if you're served ads, they're not intrusive; if you're offered "suggested videos," that you actually want to watch those videos, etc. Their goal is to make your interactions as seamless as possible so that, in essence, you never want to leave Facebook.

This is actually great for advertisers, because this approach provides multiple opportunities to advertise to people throughout the day. And by making sure that people only see ads they're actually interested in, you keep their attention focused squarely on your message.

WHAT COMPANIES SHOULD BE DOING TO ADAPT

I find that our e-commerce clients who focus on telling a story typically have much greater long-term success than those who just "sell the product." For example, I work with a company that sells juice pouches designed for very active people. It's a quick, easy snack – you sip it, get an energy boost, and are able to keep going. If you think about it, there's nothing inherently special about them – they may contain protein and electrolytes, but at the end of the day, they're just juice packs, right?

This company solved this problem by creating a story around the product. Their messaging features athletes (high school, college, and pro) talking about how and why they choose this brand and these juice packs, which builds rapport with the audience. Not to mention, an audience tends to favor your brand when they identify your product with a celebrity they already follow.

A few years ago, you could get away with just throwing a product into the feed and still get buyers (though these were mostly impulse buyers, who purchased once and didn't return). Today, that approach just won't work. Now, a brand's story, its positioning, has become far more important. The new normal involves information and transparency – at minimum, your audience wants to hear about the company's history, its team members, milestones the company's reached, the origin story, etc., in addition to being told, "Here's my product. Go buy it."

WHAT COMPANIES SHOULD STOP DOING

A lot of the people who have reached out to us for help recently are still doing what I like to call "2013 advertising": they focus on photos and text. In today's landscape, that's a mistake. Video is a much more dynamic medium, one which allows you to inject energy and excitement into your brand. Getting in front of the camera and talking to your audience about your product (or anything, really) also allows you to connect more directly with your customers.

There are, of course, exceptions. If you're a photographer or artist, using mostly still images make sense. But if you're an e-commerce brand with a variety of products and you're not telling that story or showcasing the products in a more vibrant, animated way through a video, you're not building the strongest possible relationship with potential buyers.

Without video, what you're looking at is basically an Amazon-type showcase: "Here's the product description, and here's what it looks like" (although it's worth noting that at this point, even Amazon has started including video on its platform). Customers don't just want to see photos of a product anymore – they want to hear details about it and see it in action. That's why unboxing videos do so well – even if you post a video of just your own hands unboxing your product, people will pay more attention than if you simply show them a photo of that same product.

This is one of the most important concepts that the average e-commerce store owner needs to understand. You can have a Shopify store, you can have an Amazon store, that's great; nothing wrong with that. But if you're not putting in the effort to generate creative content that will get someone to want to click, you are at a massive disadvantage compared to, say, the 19 year old who creates a Shopify store with the exact same product and is willing to jump on camera 24/7.

AN EXAMPLE OF EFFECTIVE VIDEO STRATEGY

One of my favorite strategies for using video is to create interest through a sequential series leading up to an event. Let's use a watch company as an example. Let's say a watch company has 5 models that they plan to launch on October 1.

On September 1, we would upload the first teaser video. This would be a 30-second video of the watch on a display stand that's turning in slow motion, showcasing the product. And all the video would say is, "Coming soon" and "October 1, 2018." The information is intentionally minimal – the goal is to get people talking, to get them to start asking questions on Instagram and Facebook: What's the name of this watch? How much is it going to be? When will it be available? (The answer to the last one, of course, is October 1 – there's always at least one of these, right?)

A few days later, we'd post a video of an unboxing, like a reveal. It would focus on a pair of hands opening the box, with a voice-over describing the action: trying it on, pointing out special features, etc. We'd do a separate video of this type for each of the 5 watches over the course of a month.

Then, shortly before the launch date, we would make a video featuring all 5 watches and reveal their respective costs (so first you'd see Watch 1, then its cost would appear below; the next shot would be Watch 2 followed by the reveal of its cost, etc.). Finally, all 5 watches would appear side by side with a message that's some variation of "Coming tomorrow."

This process builds anticipation and amps people up; by the time the launch date comes, there are people already wanting this product because we've been talking about it for a month.

So, to sum up: first comes the teaser video ("Coming soon"), then the unboxing, and finally the pricing/launch date reminder.

And, if you're so inclined, you could take it a step further and add extra videos where you talk about how the product came into being: where you got your inspiration, how you came up with the design, how the whole thing was conceptualized, etc. If you have original drawings of the product or the original plans, an in-depth story, or any other information that your audience might potentially find compelling, include it too. Just make sure to keep the videos short, focused, and spread out as you approach your launch date – you don't want to release more than one video per week.

You can also personalize it – on the launch day, you could post a video where you talk directly to your audience and maybe even offer them some added value; maybe something along the lines of, "Hey everyone, we have a new product coming out today. It hit stores at noon. And, because I love you guys and you're amazing, everyone who buys today gets an extra 10% off!"

You could even do a kind of live stream on the day of the launch, in the spirit of a TV shopping channel. You could talk to your customers about what's happening in real time, something like, "We just launched this thing, and orders are already coming in right now! You know, we just love the fact that so many of you are as amped about this as much as we are! Thank you for supporting us."

We've seen people do this sort of thing very successfully, simultaneously connecting with their fan base, showing their appreciation to their customers, creating a kind of group hysteria (the kind that convinces people they need to be a part of this *right now*!), and making the product launch an *event*.

FACEBOOK MESSENGER AND CHATBOTS

I haven't decided what I think about Facebook Messenger as an advertising platform yet. When Facebook first opened Messenger to advertisers – and I'm talking about them just allowing ads, before bots even came into the picture – it was great for advertisers because it gave them another way to reach their audience.

That audience, however, wasn't necessarily on board. Introducing ads angered a lot of users, who considered their Messenger feeds to be exclusively for communication with their friends, family, and colleagues; they didn't like the idea of having to scroll through ads to do so. And, when you consider how much screen space these massive banners or videos take up (especially on a phone's display), you can see how users might find that off-putting.

While I like the idea of doing a sponsored message and of having automated bots, at this point, I don't feel it's necessary to advertise in the Messenger banner slot at all. I've tested it thoroughly, and have concluded that while people do click on those ads, they do so much less frequently than in other placements. At least for the time being, the Messenger banner feels like an unnecessary second-tier ad placement that people are much more likely to simply scroll past than, say, something in the News Feed.

Of course, this could always change – after all, Messenger ads are still comparatively new, and users' reaction to them could shift in the future. Plus, you know, Facebook has to make money, right?

Chatbots are an entirely different matter. I love chatbots. I look at them as a secondary support system for stores. They allow you to make the process of communicating information to potential customers much easier. When using chatbots, instead of having to answer all the questions through an email contact form, you can write your responses right inside of Messenger. Plus, you can set up the system so that your most frequently asked questions are based on trigger words; when the bots encounter those trigger words, they can reply automatically with prepared answers, alleviating the need to have you answer every FAQ yourself.

On top of that, bots make it easy to provide information when you're offline. If a question or comment comes in when you're not available, it's extremely helpful to have something that can let the sender know, "We're not online right now, but leave your questions here, and we'll get back to you when we return." These were functions that simply weren't available on Facebook before Messenger bots came into being. There was no "vacation" or "store closed" message; the feed was just blank until you returned and answered every inquiry manually.

Bots are also a great way to introduce a product being offered for pre-sale. You can, for example, broadcast a message to your subscriber list saying, "Because you're a subscriber to our chatbot, we're giving you advance access to our new product at a special discount, 7 days before it goes public, just for being an amazing fan of our store!"

You can also use them to survey an audience before you launch. The bots let you take your product ideas right to your potential pool of buyers, and make them part of the creation process. Before you even go into production, you could send a short questionnaire to your subscribers, asking something like, "We're making a new product, and we've come up with 3 options. Here's the first one. Do you like this one, yes or no?" At the end of the survey, they'd get a message thanking them, and letting them know that their opinions will be incorporated into the final product. So in addition to providing you with some useful market research, this process also gets you an audience that has a sense of ownership and participation in the final product, which makes them much more likely to want to buy it when it launches!

Plus, if you decide to launch all three products, you now have a list of who liked what, and can segment your notification blasts accordingly – a hyper-targeted, sophisticated process that was built entirely with your bots.

Bots provide a variety of advertising opportunities, but their most important feature is that connection, that continuous communication they let you build with your customers.

But in order to really take advantage of all of the benefits that bots offer, you have to use them the right way. If they're used incorrectly, they won't help your business at all. I've subscribed to a couple of bots just to see what they were used for over the course of, say, two weeks or a month. I found that a lot of stores used their bot lists just to send a blast about a sale that's going on that day, like the way retailers used to send out email blasts (or, before that, mail flyers) for that day's sale items. Even worse, they simply repeat the message – quite a few of the stores I'd subscribed to for this experiment just broadcast sales every day, sometimes for the exact same product with an updated discount code.

Obviously, this sort of thing can start to feel very spammy. There's no value being given, there's no new information or excitement being generated, there's no direct interaction with users. Instead, they're just hammering their subscribers with sales messages. Not only is this wasting the bots' potential, it's creating an environment where people will simply auto-block or hide these messages in their feeds.

FACEBOOK'S FUTURE

Facebook will, of course, continue to make changes to their algorithms. As part of that process, I believe they'll reverse some of their current rules, and stop banning ads for certain categories. For example, I believe they'll start allowing cryptocurrency advertising soon, as there are companies in the blockchain cryptocurrency space that are offering a legitimate service that's potentially beneficial to Facebook's users.

I also believe that they'll institute stricter rules about the wording in ads. Their rules already prohibit misleading or deceptive claims or hype-y copy, but so far, they've focused their attention on broader areas (like landing pages, for instance). I get the sense that they're going to start to *really* dig into the phrasing of each individual ad.

So right now, they look at your landing pages and your funnels, and they determine whether or not what you're saying on the first page is also reflected on the second, third and fourth page in your funnel (unless they have to go past the Add to Cart or a purchase point).

I believe that it's going to get a bit little stricter, similar to when AdWords initially made that big wave of changes in their privacy policies, and a ton of accounts got shut down. Facebook's poised to do the same thing. For example, I imagine that, in the very near future, you probably won't be able to make dollar-figure profit claims in your ads (in the sense of, "I made 6 figures off of this thing!"). Facebook is obviously very protective of its brand, and to that end, new restrictions are introduced regularly. So far, it's happened every year and each time, it's become harder and harder to deploy an ad.

While rising costs can be problematic for advertisers, higher prices do favor those who are serious about Facebook advertising. A more expensive advertising environment tends to weed out those who aren't willing to continuously test and figure out what works for their industries, and to adapt when the Facebook landscape changes.

Advertisers who are committed to doing these things have a long-term strategy in place, and aren't particularly concerned about Facebook's ad costs. Are these costs going up? Absolutely. But then, I have clients who have been getting some of the cheapest clicks and leads they've ever experienced in the last couple years.

What I'm getting at is that you simply have to make better ads. If you make an effort to find ways to connect with more people, no matter your business's niche or industry, you'll be just fine.

Those are the policy changes I see happening at Facebook in the near future. In terms of new features and functions, Facebook will soon include mid-roll ad placement (advertisements that pop up in the middle of videos), adding another option to the already-standard pre- and post-roll ads. This is something you've already experienced on YouTube, where they intersperse a longer-form video with short ads – like mini commercial breaks.

And a bit further down the pipeline, advertising on AR (augmented reality) and VR (virtual reality) devices will be incorporated as well. The rapid increase in the VR and AR market in recent years will soon make this technology mainstream. As it becomes more affordable, the number of adopters will increase dramatically, and Facebook will find ways to monetize the trend.

Then, of course, there's Facebook Watch – once the public fully embraces that, you'll be able to advertise on someone's TV show during a commercial break; however, unlike traditional TV commercials, Facebook will make it possible to focus your ads very strategically to the audience that's most likely to be interested in your products.

ADAPTING TO FACEBOOK TRENDS TO INCREASE PERFORMANCE

If you keep a close eye on Facebook's new initiatives and prepare your business to incorporate them into your marketing strategy, you're always ready to take advantage of all kinds of new advertising opportunities.

For example, Facebook is starting to put a lot of capital and attention into video series, particularly ones featuring various Facebook celebrities. Since this is something that Facebook is focusing on at the moment – really committing a lot of time and attention to it – that's your cue to focus your energies on it as well. Start putting together your own video series, featuring your product, or your company, or an interesting employee – whatever works. Clearly, this is what Facebook is looking for, and you want to do your best to give it to them, ideally producing enough volume and frequency of content that they'll start promoting you on their own.

Facebook has a lot riding on the Watch platform, and they're promoting it non-stop. They've even had commercials on traditional TV! They're basically waving a big, neon sign that screams, "Participate in Facebook Watch!" For advertisers, this should be an "Aha!" moment. They should immediately start thinking, "Maybe I need to create some video. Perhaps a series that releases new episodes every day, or every week. Possibly, I should plan multiple seasons of this series."

And while you're doing this, maybe start planning how you'll incorporate a VR/AR strategy into your future plans. Facebook may have stopped talking about it recently, but that doesn't mean they've given up on the idea. They're just waiting for the optimal time to refocus their attention. With that in mind, it would be smart to keep a finger on the pulse of the industry, so that you can be prepared when Facebook adds it to the platform. It might not happen for a while – maybe years – but if you at least understand the technology and what's happening in the industry, you'll be able to hit the ground running when it arrives.

And let's not forget, Facebook will adapt with cryptocurrencies, and they will adapt with other technology as it comes as well. When a company introduces a new platform or product, Facebook's already aware of it. If it's worthwhile, they're going to find a way to assimilate it. It's like when they introduced an integrated payment system that allowed Facebook friends to transfer money to each other in Messenger – this was, of course, modeled on PayPal, Venmo, and other, similar apps. As soon as those apps became available, Facebook said, "We can do the same thing," and then went ahead and did it.

So basically, just stay aware of what they're adding to their network, and figure out how you can take advantage of it for your own business.

Also, it's a good idea to keep in mind that Facebook's primary goal is to make it so users never have to leave the site. Previously, when you clicked on a product, the Facebook page would redirect you to an external store on another platform, and you would pay through the store's payment page. Recently, however, Facebook has streamlined the process, making for a much more seamless interaction.

Sellers can now build an e-commerce store right on Facebook, and customers can order and check out right in the Facebook store. This is great in terms of convenience for the customer, and it benefits the store owner as well: Facebook charges significantly less for views and engagements when links redirect to locations within the Facebook ecosystem; when links send users off-site, it can triple (or even quadruple) these costs.

MY TOP 3 STRATEGIES FOR GENERATING E-COMMERCE SALES

Strategy 1:

I've already mentioned the first one, but it's worth repeating: you have to start generating videos featuring your product. Whether that takes the form of unboxing your own product (acting like it's the first time you've ever seen it), interacting with the product, or getting it to influencers, the important thing is to get those videos out there. Trends show that people love experiencing unboxing videos with you.

You can be the first person to introduce your product to the world, then send it off to a couple of Instagram or YouTube influencers to do the same thing (with the added bonus of getting the influencers' feedback on the product as well). This will allow you to build a huge awareness of the product before it even comes out.

History proves that this works – think about those technology bloggers who get access to a new phone before it's out on the market. They review and promote that phone, breaking down the features, how it feels, how it interacts with apps, and all the other details that makes the phone special. This not only builds product awareness, it generates anticipation, and helps potential consumers feel more knowledgeable and secure about their future purchase. So take advantage of the benefits, and do the same thing with your own product – it works!

Strategy 2:

Retargeting is extremely important to get buyers to your store. Telling your customer, "Y'all come back now!" isn't enough – the bare minimum won't get you the results you want. Instead, implement a system of sequential retargeting.

Here's an example of sequential retargeting: let's say, for example, you've been showcasing a product for 7 days. Members of your audience have already seen the product; they've put it into their carts, but haven't actually made the purchase yet. Rather than just feeding them the same "reminder" ad ("Hey, you forgot something!"), you could take a more tailored approach.

For instance, you could set up different sales points or sales windows based on a custom audience in your Facebook and/or Instagram account. Let's say that, for the first 3 days of the retargeting effort, you offer these people a 15% discount. You could say, "This is a limited-time opportunity… this sale will be over soon," without necessarily specifying an exact time frame. Then, once that 3-day window is over, you could replace that sale with another short-term one: let's say from days 4 to 6, you lower the discount from 15% to 10%.

What will end up happening is, the people who remember that 15% sale are going to message you and say, "Hey, there was a 15% sale a few days ago. Can I get the code from that ad?"

The first thing you'll do is to add these people to a bot list that you've built, because they went to the trouble of reaching out to you, so they're obviously interested in what you're selling. Second, you give them the 15% off: "Since you reached out to me about this, I'm happy to extend the offer – here's the code!"

The result? Now you have another bunch of direct contacts, and you've built goodwill with a group of grateful customers.

Now, let's say that Day 6 has elapsed, and you have customers that still haven't completed their purchases. You could send out another notification saying something like, "This is your final opportunity to get this product at a discounted rate." Again, you don't specify what the discount is; you just provide a generic coupon code. It could be the same 10%, it could go down to 5% – whatever you prefer.

Besides getting those sales, the goal of this process is to examine which sales points within those windows people respond to most favorably. What pushes them over the edge? Is it a higher discount? Is it the fact that they might be missing out on something? Or is it that they're procrastinators, and just realized that you meant it when you said, "Hey, this is your last chance?" Based on who responds to what and when, you can start to more accurately figure out what prompts people to purchase your product in general, as well as what sales strategy is likely to get a response out of each individual in this new customer list.

This does take some time and energy to set up and analyze, but it's definitely worth the effort.

Strategy 3:

Further expounding on Strategy 1: start telling your story with a video series, where you release a new video every week. Just start creating. Facebook is rewarding brands that create regular and consistent content. I've noticed that those of my clients who are releasing new content weekly have been getting cheaper clicks, cheaper CPMs, and cheaper leads. Over time, I'm noticing my deliverability is just naturally getting better, I'm seeing that people are engaging with our content more often.

When the algorithms started changing, Facebook mentioned that organic reach would decline. We've already witnessed that. We get it – it's a pay-to-play platform now. But advertising is significantly more impactful when coupled with engaging, relevant content. So no matter what's happening in Facebook at any given moment, it's always in your company's best interests to have a portion of your advertising budget earmarked for content creation.

I've also noticed that *our* costs for a variety of elements – especially lead acquisition – are going down as the audience notices that we release new videos so frequently. It doesn't have to be complicated; even a 1- or 2-minute video does the job. You could strategize these out months in advance, and have a whole library of them ready to go.

This is probably the easiest of the 3 strategies to implement right away, since it's just making a few videos to help people understand your brand, and to get them engaged.

These strategies work synergistically – they can (and should!) be mixed-and-matched. Let's say you're doing that weekly video series as a behind-the-scenes kind of thing: the production cycle, how the company makes its decisions, how you go about creating new products, things of that nature. When you retarget those viewers, you can create different segments based on how long they viewed. Some people will watch 3 seconds; others will watch 5%, or 10%, all the way up to 95%. The 95% viewers are the ones who are probably going to end up buying a lot of your stuff because they're the most engaged.

In this way, you create a custom audience, and direct your video series right to them. And based on the percentage of that content that they viewed, you can determine how to appeal to them. Do you send these people a product? Do you send them to another video? How do you capitalize on their interest?

I typically divide this group at the 75% point (those who watched 75% or more of a video, and those who watched less than 75%). The 75%-and-over crowd can be directed towards your other products because they're the most engaged. You also want to reward them for being avid viewers of your show. You can meet both goals by retargeting this group to your best sellers, saying, "Hey, we've noticed you've been watching our shows. As a token of our appreciation, we want to give you first dibs on getting 25% off the best-selling product of your choice." You get additional sales, and they get a bonus for their patronage.

Your goal for the under-75% viewers is to keep feeding them more content until they get to the 75% or more point. You can try different topics and formats to figure out what it would take to get their percentages up. The fact that they watch even a small portion is a good sign – it means they're at least somewhat interested – and if you keep nurturing that, keep providing new videos at a regular rate, eventually more and more of them will convert to the 75%-and-over group.

*Do you want to see how we have a 1500+ Return on Adspend in a competitive E-Commerce market? You can learn how to get back $15 for every $1 spend on Facebook Ads by going to **www.cvoaccel.com/success.***

CHAPTER 3

Enrico Lugnan: The Instagram Whisperer

I'm Enrico Lugnan, a 25-year-old Italian guy who loves strategy! I'm the co-founder and CSO of Avenik, a social media marketing agency that helps brands and corporations to craft and execute their social media marketing and sales strategy.

We started in social media around two years ago, grew an Instagram network from 0 to 8 million followers within the first year, and then expanded into the area of strategy. We've been helping companies to craft and execute strategies for the past 12 months.

As we started to help other companies, we found that a lot of them seem to be really attached to the way they've done their marketing in the past, and only use social media marketing assets in a very limited way, mostly sticking to very basic campaigns. They are used to more passive marketing tools (like Google AdWords and Facebook in the early days) and to relying on retargeting, rather than proactively crafting content to find their target audiences.

At first, we were unaware of this problem. We simply assumed that most companies already knew how to incorporate social media effectively. But after interfacing with them, talking with quite a few of them, we realized that the strategic part – the process of coming up with a campaign and figuring out how to structure it – was actually a big pain point for a lot of companies.

For example, from our perspective, Instagram and Facebook are two sides of the same coin. We use Instagram for the marketing aspect and Facebook Ads for the sales aspect. By doing this, we are able to test the reactions to the content on Instagram, finding out what type of audience and what types of pages actually provide the best results. Then, with all the targeting options you have on Facebook (the Facebook pixel, plus all the custom events and conversions available to you), you're actually able to retarget with amazing accuracy.

There were a lot of companies that just relied on the detailed targeting on Facebook alone. So, for instance, if one of these was a sports product company, they just looked for users who had an interest in sports and assumed that would be sufficient. If it didn't work, the company would assume that it was because their product is wrong for Facebook Ads, when the actual problem was a combination of bad creative (e.g. the ads looked like something pulled straight out of 1997) and incorrect or insufficient targeting.

We tested it, and found that if you have really good laser targeting – not based on assumption, but based on real data (historical data, even Google AdWords data) – you can actually reach your target audience even if the creative isn't great, and you can get a positive ROI (even if it's only *slightly* positive) pretty easily on Facebook.

TIPS FOR LEVERAGING FACEBOOK AND INSTAGRAM

The first thing we tell all the clients who come to us – regardless of whether it's for help with Facebook Ads, e-commerce, retargeting, optimizing content, or creating an Instagram account and actually selling merchandise – is not to start with sales. Inevitably, their first reaction is, "But I want the ROI!"

Our response is, "Of course, but you have to build a kind of trust and an infrastructure first."

That's not to say that a company couldn't get sales right away. It's entirely possible to make $100K in 30 days with an e-commerce store selling, say, fidget spinners – that happens. But we don't advise this business model, because you want to get an ROI that lasts longer than 30 days (or however long that initial bump lasts before it dies out).

Instead, we build an infrastructure where there is a constant flow of targeted traffic, and based on the overall behavior of the targeted traffic (not on a single aspect like gender, device, frequency, average time on website, or any of the other parameters that analytics tools like Facebook, Google Analytics, etc. provide), proactively use the data to reach out to more targeted cold traffic. Plus, we always have an engagement campaign running – not just conversion, not just traffic, but an engagement campaign that has nothing to do with sales whatsoever.

To give you an example, let's take a recent client of ours who sells interior design pieces. The standard approach would have been an ROI for a Facebook ad campaign, just to demonstrate that we can deliver good ROI with consistent growth in the first 60 days.

But we wanted to take a different approach because it's worked for us before, and as a bonus, this client actually understood the benefits of long-term ROI over short-term ROI. So we built up an Instagram account. For the record, we already knew how to manage Instagram – we mastered the Instagram platform first, then expanded into Facebook Ads.

So we built an Instagram account that reached around 11,000 followers in the first two months. Based on that, we knew what type of content worked best, what type of interior design images worked best, and most importantly, what type of influencers worked best. And I'm not talking about the overpriced, 200K-verified accounts that sell bikinis; I'm talking about the 45-year-old housewife from Norway who truly loves interior design. We talked to around 25 influencers of this kind, shipped products to them, received a really awesome response and great feedback, and confirmed the viability of the product with actual people in the industry. This was incredibly useful information – after all, I'm not an interior design expert so I have no idea which product might work best.

So we reviewed the responses, and realized that there were 4 or 5 items that everyone was choosing, while the remaining 14 didn't draw any interest. We shipped those 4 to 5 items to the influencers, took the user-generated content from them, and created a carousel campaign with the 5 top-selling items. We didn't choose them; we didn't even sell them. We just delivered the options to them, and let the market choose the products.

We then put those 5 products in a carousel ad, generated a bit of traffic, populated the pixel, started a retargeting and lookalike, and that was it – job done!

Over the course of a week, we got a consistent 9.8x ROI (i.e. 980% ROI), and the first 48-hours that we launched the website from Instagram, just from our profile (not from the influencers or anything), we had to run 380 clicks.

I can attest that this strategy works. I've only tried it a few times, but it worked brilliantly every time.

IDENTIFYING INFLUENCERS ON INSTAGRAM

If you want to go into influencer marketing, ideally, you produce your own products or you're doing private labeling (or you have access to a small sample of products); if you have a purely drop shipping business, it will be a bit harder to do influencer marketing (unless your products are custom items or in specific niches).

Before doing influencer marketing, we typically ship samples of the products to between 20 and 50 influencers, just to gather data. First, this gets you 20-50 pieces of content for free (so you don't have to pay for the creative), and they usually deliver good content. Second, if an influencer really likes the product, she might tag you more than once, even if you only agreed on one tag initially. You could simply send her a discount code; possibly something like, "If you purchase, I'll give you 50% off on your next order plus a 10% discount to your followers," and try to start that kind of relationship.

But if you're not able to do that, you really need to rely on good old analytics. Of course, you don't have analytics for Instagram (there's no function for seeing impressions, or the PPC, or the customer acquisition cost), but you *do* have access to the number of likes, the number of comments, and the number of followers. Additionally, websites like SocialBlade can tell you whether and by how much your followers are growing (or not growing). Then you can add some stats by manually checking the last 20 posts, likes, and comments, calculating ratios and factoring in statistical data. Through this process, you can figure out which influencers are performing better than the others. When we have a list of the ones that are performing the best, we deliver the products to them. It can take a bit of time and effort – before finding 25 influencers for our most recent campaign, we analyzed 300 accounts.

BUILDING RELATIONSHIPS WITH INFLUENCERS

When we first contact influencers, we don't reach out to them like an agency; we just connect with them like regular people. We don't try to start a business relationship initially; we simply send a message saying something like, "Hey, I like your page. We have a product. I think you might actually like the product. If you want the product, I'm willing to ship it for a shout-out." It's pretty straightforward – just a DM and an email and that's it. If they reply, they reply; if they don't, we move on.

With micro-influencers, with people who have built smaller networks, this approach works well. A few months ago, the micro-influencer cutoff was under 50,000 followers. Since then, Instagram's grown really fast, so at this point, that number is more like under 100,000 followers – within that range, you can reasonably reach out to them directly like this. And if they have a really engaged audience, even a 10K account can actually provide 10 sales with one shout-out, as long as the product is on target and make sense for them to promote.

FACEBOOK ADVERTISING TRENDS IN 2019

An upcoming/soon-to-be trend is Facebook chatbots with engagement campaigns, with content marketing campaigns. I'm not talking about using Facebook chatbots to sell; I mean Facebook chatbots being used in a customer support capacity and as a content marketing platform (like, say, an engaging newsletter, which used to be a very effective content marketing device before the advent of the email marketing network).

Given chatbots' open rates and click-through rates, if you base it on actual engagement from a post (not a message campaign or a lead magnet campaign – just pure engagement and pure value), I think that's going to be huge. Although not for everyone – I know some people won't adopt it, because it's one of those strategies that requires more than a few weeks to deliver ROI. But the companies that adopt this implementation effectively will make a good ROI, largely because of the 30% open rate.

WHAT COMPANIES SHOULD BE DOING TO ADAPT

The most important concept that companies need to understand is that pure-sales advertising is dying, and there's nothing they can do to stop it. That's just a shift of the market, of the culture, and of the nature of the medium. It's like television advertising – in the '80s, they had ads on TV that were just really sales-y. Then over time, all of that sales-y advertisement got shifted to the low-rated channels that no one watches. That's the same shift that's happening in Facebook Ads.

This is why influencer marketing works so well on Instagram. It never worked on Facebook, because Facebook became overcrowded, noisy, and kind of spammy as it aged. While Instagram is a content-based platform (which means that you can still find the right content from the right influencers even now, several years after its launch), Facebook is more of a comment-based platform, so content isn't really king the way it is on Instagram. That said, you can still get equally good content based results with Facebook Ads if you approach it the right way – if you're able to do the right retargeting with the right ad with the right type of content, that's all you really need.

I'm not trying to say that Instagram is the best platform, but I see that the real value is in content, and right now, Instagram is the best content-driven platform. YouTube is also a content-driven platform, but like Facebook, YouTube got really crowded. It's really competitive, and sometimes it's harder to scroll through YouTube to find the content, because the YouTube algorithm doesn't really help you to find the content you might be interested in; it's more about monetization ads. Plus, it has in-stream video ads, which don't really exist on Instagram.

One of the smartest things that both Facebook and Instagram are doing is making sure that the ads on their respective platforms look and feel exactly like the posts. So if I scroll quickly through Instagram, I don't notice the ads at all. Instagram Stories is, in my opinion, the most seamless. If I see an ad in Instagram Stories, it looks like an Instagram Story – in order to be approved, the ad has to be 15 seconds long, and to have the same structure and feel as any other Instagram story. I think that's why the platform is growing – because it's pure content, and in order to get approved and to perform, the ads need to have good content as well.

WHAT COMPANIES SHOULDN'T BE DOING IN 2019

As Instagram grew in the last six months – and also at the time when Facebook was booming – companies weren't really able to keep up organically, so they started faking it. They started buying fake followers: first on Twitter, then on

Facebook, now on Instagram. Those are simply vanity metrics, and a real company with a real framework in a real long-term business with a good business model shouldn't rely on vanity metrics.

What matters at the end of the month (depending on the business model you have) is return on ad spend, customer acquisition cost, lifetime value – definitely not the number of likes or of followers. The impulse is understandable – it seems reasonable to think that when you buy followers, you gain social proof, but that's actually completely wrong; that's not how the algorithm works. In fact, it can work against you, so it's best to avoid anything fake on a content- and engagement-driven platform. And you should also avoid anyone that recommends faking anything.

FACEBOOK MESSENGER AND CHATBOTS

The strategic advantage of a Messenger chatbot is significantly shorter response time. If you know your target audience and you know your product, ideally, you should also know the main 5-15 questions an audience member is likely to have about that product. 95% of the time, customer support is answering the same set of questions over and over, and you can create a chatbot that provides a chosen set of answers to these questions, based on the customer's selections.

If you use the chatbot for engagement and customer service (instead of using them to push sales, or for giving customers a discount code, then another discount coupon, followed by another discount code), you not only differentiate yourself; *you also actually help customers.* So when someone reaches out to you and says, "I want to buy the product but I have a problem," there's a good chance that the bot you set up will be able to answer any questions he has right in the moment.

The opening response can be anything: *What problem are you having? How can I help you? Do you want to schedule a call?*

You can integrate scheduling a call (and a number of other utilities) with the Messenger bot. If you're familiar with ManyChat and Zapier, you can basically automatically parse the data that the bot conversations provide without the need for any further tools. You can, for example, collect emails, enter them into a Google sheet, then use Zapier to move them from your Google sheet to your active campaigns, and then from the Google sheet and active campaign to your

Calendly, and end up with everything – from booking to scheduling the call to creating the Zoom or Uberconference link – connected, without employing any other apps. You set up your chatbot once, prospective customers reach out to you, they click the right set of options, and you have a call with them within 24 hours. It's pretty amazing - even companies that have real people doing this aren't really able to manage it effectively within 24 hours, but a chatbot can.

FACEBOOK ADVERTISING THROUGHOUT 2019

This can be tricky to predict, because the development of Facebook Ads and the trends depend on how many users actually apply best practices and make an effort not to ruin the platform.

Like for example, the reason that Facebook is prohibiting ICOs (and just about anything else related to cryptocurrency) in the latest update is that, when it was allowed, it was pretty seriously abused. People came onboard with get-rich-quick schemes, fake ICOs, and illegal white papers. Obviously, Facebook doesn't want to incur the legal problems associated with this sort of thing; nor do they want to have users leave and/or to have the platform ruined by bad advertising.

Assuming that everyone starts using the platform the right way (i.e. the way it was meant to be used), Facebook will gradually start to lift some of the restrictions. The advertising platform and overall strategy have been slowly heading in an interaction-based (as opposed to a purely call-to-action-based) direction. I believe that this will continue – I see Facebook remaining an interaction-based platform within social media for the foreseeable future, but I think that the tools Facebook adds will become a lot more content-based.

Right now, if you have a blog or a podcast and you don't have a Facebook ad strategy, you're losing big-time! If you do these types of content pieces well enough, they can pretty much do the selling for you! So if you have a blog and/or a podcast, you should absolutely be distributing it/them through Facebook Ads.

So I think that if everyone uses best practices and uses the platform as it's meant to be used, rather than approaching it as a get-rich-quick scheme (which never works), I think Facebook's future is going to be filled with a lot more content.

HOW COMPANIES CAN MAINTAIN (OR EVEN INCREASE) PERFORMANCE IN 2019

The best way for companies to ensure that they continue to do well is to keep gathering data about their ideal customer. They have to develop a progressively deeper and deeper understanding of that customer. Once you're able to do that, you're also able to create the right content for your ideal audience. You need to have the right reach, the right number of impressions – 10,000 impressions is all you need if they're all the right ones. So if you actually target your content and you're continuously researching – don't stop! Don't think that, just because you have enough customers at the moment, you know everything about them – try to go deeper and keep split-testing and split-testing and split-testing. You're not going to see results in two weeks; it's not going to give you an ROI in six weeks. But ideally, six months from now, every ad you run is going to 10x your ad spend (i.e. 1,000% ROI).

STRATEGIES TO FURTHER IDENTIFY CUSTOMER DATA

First of all, you have to put yourself in the position of actually understanding the data. I'm not talking about having a data analyst or someone condense things for you – you have to actually understand what all of it means yourself. You need to understand why, for example, if frequency goes up, your cost per click might go up.

You need to understand the concepts your business is built upon for yourself. If you are the producer of the product, or if you're someone who believes in the product, and you know where you want to go with this (i.e. you're not just focusing on where you are right now; you're actually thinking about where you want to be 10 steps from now), you should have a first-hand understanding of the data. A data analyst can understand what the information means in a given spreadsheet, but he can't see how it relates to your overall big picture.

Second, don't make assumptions about your clients – let the data guide you instead. For instance, a while ago, we got a consulting call from a company that sold high-end lingerie. They were unhappy about the fact that a lot of the influencers we were using had mostly-male audiences, when they needed a female audience (because, of course, the end users for lingerie are women). We tried to make them understand that the influencers who showcase things like lingerie are usually models or model types, and there aren't a lot of women who would respond positively to that.

Yes, a large portion of their market consists of women who love the product and buy it because they love it, but I'm pretty sure that the impulse buyer in that specific market is a man, a guy who imagines his wife, girlfriend, or fiancé – whoever he's buying that gift for – in that outfit, thinks, "Okay, I want her to look like that," and then buys the product.

We tried to explain that, but they didn't really trust us or believe in this concept, so they stopped buying the shout-outs from the influencers. They were not our client in terms of management and sales – they were just trying to look for a consultation – so we didn't push the issue. But all those influencers they stopped buying from kept on selling those same types of ads to other companies, and the ads continued to be successful.

That's the point of data – it shows you when and where you might go wrong. You might have made a wrong assumption at some point, and that wrong assumption kept going and compounding, and ended up ruining your understanding of the client, potentially making your marketing efforts ineffectual. That's why you need to keep split testing and gathering data and gathering data and gathering data.

TOP 3 STRATEGIES FOR E-COMMERCE COMPANIES

A couple of years ago, companies that understood that Facebook Ads were a blue ocean got a lot of return. Unfortunately, that's not Facebook anymore – there's no more blue ocean to be found there. But it can still be profitable.

The first strategy is purely for Facebook sales, and involves a Facebook content marketing funnel. Start a funnel based on engagement, retargeting based on the people that engaged (as well as the corresponding lookalike audience). Next, refine the type of audience, trying to go from engagement to traffic, then from traffic to specific custom conversions based on your funnel. Throughout the process, keep delivering content that will ensure that people will associate the type or category of product you sell with your brand. If you're able to do that, you can make it so that your brand becomes synonymous with that product in the customer's mind.

Another strategy that's worked really well is one I mentioned earlier – connecting micro-influencer marketing with Facebook Ads. Micro-influencer marketing will help you generate the first wave of traffic and the first set of data, which you can then retarget using all the data that Facebook extracts from this group for you.

You can also think about other tools – there are a lot of remarketing tools that are outside Facebook Ads, but which can use the Facebook ad pixel (like AdRoll, Connectio, etc.). Depending on what you want to accomplish, using these tools strategically can dramatically improve your results.

The third strategy – and this is something that we work on with our biggest clients – is to start acting like a media company. If you sell a product that's, say, in the fishing niche, try to become the go-to expert on fishing. Design your content strategy around the idea of becoming the main distributor of valuable content within that niche. Whether it's blog posts, podcasts, Instagram pages, Facebook pages, a YouTube channel, or any other distribution medium, you have to become the authority in the field.

This used to be the domain of special-interest magazines, but magazines no longer control the market. Last year in the U.S., Facebook ad spend was around $20 billion; the total ad spend on print in the U.S. – not just for newspaper; *all* print ads – was about the same.

So, going back to the example above, while fishing magazines may still exist, they're no longer the go-to reference, because no one between the ages of 14 and 34 really buys magazines anymore. So you can become the new media version of that magazine. It's costly – that's definitely one of the more expensive strategies out there. But if you have the budget and expertise to do it, you potentially have a unicorn business on your hands.

POTENTIAL LONGEVITY OF THESE TIPS AND STRATEGIES

All of the strategies and suggestions I mentioned here are based on the current content paradigms and the current market. So if the content changes and/or the market changes, you have to change. Using micro-influencers works well right now, but it might not work six months from now. That's why it's so important to keep split-testing and gathering data.

That said, unless something drastic happens – like something really, truly weird that majorly disrupt the existing market – I think these strategies will work really well for at least the next 24 months.

CHAPTER 4

Janak Mehta: Facebook Ad Ninja

I'm Janak Mehta. I've been an internet marketer and strategist for over a decade, and Facebook advertising is my favorite discussion topic!

I grew up in India, and got my Masters in Information Networking at Carnegie Mellon University. After that, I went to work for Bell Communication Research Lab, then on to the Ford Motor Company.

During this period, I also started a real estate investment business. From 2004 to 2007, the company turned over a high volume of properties – over an 18-month period, we had turned over $2.4 million dollars' worth of holdings, and at one point we owned 80 properties.

I felt like I was living the American dream, like I was doing what I'd come to this country to do.

And then the recession hit, and we lost everything, literally – all the properties were gone. That was a huge wake-up call for me. I realized that, while the real estate game had been interesting, it was too unstable – there were too many factors involved that were outside of my control. I also felt a pull to return to my more "technical" roots.

Prior to the economic downturn, I'd spent several years studying marketing in order to apply those skills to the real estate business. I attended quite a few internet marketing seminars between 2003 and 2005. Although I didn't have a marketing background, I was fascinated by it. So after I decided to leave real estate behind, I turned my attention to the marketing field, and decided to follow that interest to see where it led.

So I learned everything I could and implemented this new knowledge, then learned and implemented some more. I quickly got a sense of what works and what doesn't, and in 2007, I launched a marketing agency. We really did everything under the sun: SEO, Google AdWords, other paid traffic strategy, content marketing, etc. By 2014, the company had grown and we were doing well, but I felt like we were concentrating on too many areas, spreading ourselves too thin and not really focusing our efforts effectively.

Around this time, I read a book called *Built to Sell*, which talked about how to advertise your service-based company. That book led me to change the direction of my business completely, convincing me to focus on a single service, which would allow us to offer our customers a more comprehensive level of expertise. The platform we chose was Facebook Ads.

Clearly, this was the right decision, because ever since we made the switch, the company has been growing like crazy! Since we changed our focus, we've doubled in size and revenue every year. We now have 8 people working for us – it's a small staff, but we all love what we do. We typically focus on two niches: what we call "experts" and – my favorite! – e-commerce.

E-commerce is where we have bigger budgets, with clients that spend hundreds of thousands – or even millions – of dollars. We get to experiment a lot, and, since every client has different needs and goals, we get to significantly deepen our understanding of the medium as we work on our clients' various campaigns.

2019 TRENDS IN FACEBOOK ADVERTISING

One of the biggest trends we've seen so far going into 2019 is a massive increase in the use of video ads.

Facebook is definitely giving preferential treatment to posts featuring videos, both from an organic and a paid standpoint. There are a lot of amazing benefits that come with the use of video ads on Facebook – among other things, they're excellent for building a brand, and they allow you to really showcase a product and all its inherent benefits.

Video ads are here to stay, and are actually going to increase in importance in the foreseeable future. A recent statistic indicated that Facebook's 2.2 billion-strong monthly active user base is watching over 100 million hours of video a day. And demand is only expected to increase over time.

Another major recent trend that I feel very strongly about is dynamic product ads. Dynamic product ads are basically retargeting on steroids. What Facebook has allowed us to do is upload our inventory on Facebook – essentially, create a product feed – and Facebook then targets your ad to people who have visited your competitors' sites. So, instead of the standard "Targeting 101" approach (you bring traffic to your website and then you follow it wherever it goes), dynamic product ads let you get inside your competitors' territory (of course, that means they can target your audience too, but if you approach this strategically, you can still get it to work out in your favor).

Dynamic product ads work. In regular retargeting, the typical ROI averages 12x ad spend (i.e. advertising expenditure). Compare that to dynamic product ads, which can have an ROI of 36x – 40x ad spend. We're looking at potentially huge numbers – there's a big difference between getting $12 for every $1 invested vs. getting $36 back for that same $1, right? Now, that doesn't happen for every campaign, especially when you have a campaign at scale. But generally speaking, as long as you make sure that the product is relevant to your audience, you should get great results with dynamic product ads.

Also, Facebook has different types of ads that allow you to use different modalities. I've found the current trend of retargeting on carousel ads to be really effective. Carousel ads allow you to have a single ad featuring multiple images and headlines, which you can use to tell a story or showcase a variety of product offers.

Another trend we've been testing, and have been getting good results with, is chatbots. We use ManyChat, but there are plenty of other chatbot software companies out there, like SegMate, Opesta, and Chatfuel. Whichever version you use, the goal here is to extend your communication beyond email. This is important for a couple of reasons: first, the chatbot message open rate is significantly higher than for email messages. Second, chatbots allow you to automate the process of responding to and following up on basic questions that your audience poses.

A word of caution about this particular development – while you should definitely implement the chatbot trend while it's trending, keep a close eye on the audience response to it. I believe that over time, marketers ruin all platforms, and given chatbots' current popularity, I'm guessing they're going to develop a bad reputation pretty soon. We've probably got 2-2.5 years where these chatbots will provide a solid ROI, but after that, as far as Facebook users are concerned, they'll go the way of email. Current email open rates, generally speaking, are less than 10%, and chatbots will eventually be the same.

The last trend we're in the process of testing is the automated bidding platform. We've implemented this in a lot of our clients' campaigns, and seen tremendous ability to scale very, very quickly. For example, one of our clients in the tech industry had a product launch, and needed to generate 100,000 leads for it. Using automated bidding platforms, we were able to generate those leads in about 4 days, for about $125,000.

There are several automatic bidding platforms, including Companion Labs and Leadza, as well as several other tools that help with budget allocation, so campaign budget optimization is also critical.

USING VIDEO ADS EFFECTIVELY

Normally, you create a video ad, and then build the audience behind the scenes yourself. One of the brilliant things about Facebook is that it actually builds audiences for you, based on how much of each video people watch.

To take advantage of this function, first, you'll obviously need to create a video! It should be somewhere from 3 to 5 minutes long. Make sure the content of this video is relevant to your audience, then market it to them.

Once it's out there and being viewed, Facebook tracks how many people have watched the video and for how long, then separates them into various lists accordingly. Some people might watch the video for, let's say, 10 seconds; others will watch 25% or 50% or 75%, all the way up to 100% of the video, and Facebook will create a separate list for each group based on consumption percentage.

Then, you can take the list of people who watched, say, over 75% of the video, and target them to the top of the funnel. You can redirect them to your landing page (that has an offer on it), or to a product category page, or even to a specific product page. The idea here is, the more of the content they've consumed, the more interested they are, and the more likely they are to purchase. So the video ads become a resource for building the audience, retargeting, conversion, and lead generation as well, and it works beautifully.

CHATBOTS AND MESSENGER

I love that Facebook allows us to run ads where we can actually talk directly to our audience via Messenger and chatbots. They make it much easier to do business, and to connect with customers. If they're managed carefully, these new platforms have incredible potential. Even now, we are implementing it for our clients, and we are seeing great results in terms of cost per acquisition.

However, it's *really* important to make sure that the medium doesn't end up getting abused. My concern is that, as these become the hot new trend, they'll get turned into another "me too!" info strategy, with a lot of people jumping on the bandwagon just because it's there. Inevitably, this will cause the effectiveness to go down.

So I would advise caution in implementing this tool. Nonetheless, for now at least, you should absolutely be using bots – just use them the right way. Think of them as tools that allow you to communicate with your prospects in a modality that's different from email. When users interact with your chatbot (asking questions, clicking on links and buttons, etc.), the chatbot will capture their email as well as provide the information they seek, which gives you the ability to broadcast, for example, a newsletter to them through Facebook Messenger while also communicating with them through email. That's very powerful because they're going to look at it right away, and most of them will then take some action.

So, from that standpoint, chatbots are great! Just make sure, when you're implementing them, that you're thinking about the entire customer experience. It's not just about the sale; it's about communicating effectively with your audience before, during, and after the sale.

Also, I strongly recommend using marketing automation tools like Klaviyo, Infusionsoft, ActiveCampaign, etc. to replicate some of the same funnels and follow-up that you already use for your email lists, and implement them in your chatbot as well. This will result in much better engagement from your content production.

So, again, for the time being, I love chatbots; however, I'm cautious about making them a major part of my strategy. At the moment, they're great. But, given their potential to become overused (and potentially irritating to Facebook's users), I wouldn't suggest choosing chatbots long-term in place of the tried-and-true tools and strategies that have been proven to work over the past years.

Instead, I believe that chatbots work best when they're used in conjunction with (and as support for) other communication tools. For example, we have a client for whom we're implementing a strategy around birthdays. So, we captured the birthdays of everyone in their audience, and sent a $100 off coupon (valid for the subsequent month) to everyone who has a birthday coming up within the next seven days. We send these coupons via broadcast messages in Messenger, through email, and also target them with Facebook ads. In other words, we are using this strategy to engage more with the audience and their special occasions. This approach has successfully generated sales, so we've concluded that this is an effective strategy.

DYNAMIC PRODUCT ADS

As I said, I'm a big fan of dynamic product ads – their potential ROI is amazing. In order to maximize their effectiveness, you need to have an understanding of your metrics: your cost per acquisition and cost per click, conversion rates, customer lifetime value, etc.

Second, what we call "seasoning the pixel". You need to have a lot of traffic driven at every conversion stage: not just at the top of the funnel, but the middle and the bottom as well. This will ensure that you're giving your business enough focus on converting repeat business through upsells or downsells. You want to aim for a minimum of 25 conversions per week.

A brief overview of funnels

The top of the funnel is where you build awareness of your product. For an e-commerce client, some examples of the top of a funnel would be a landing page, a category page, or in certain cases, some sort of consumers' guide – basically, just a free, irresistible offer (aka a "lead magnet" in marketing terms).

The middle of the funnel is where you help customers evaluate their needs to select between options. This could take the form of, say, a quiz to figure out which model of a product would suit them best. In an e-commerce setting, this would be the product page or the sales page.

The bottom of the funnel (or "down the funnel") is where conversions happen. This could include everything from explaining why your product is the best, to guiding people who've already added something to their carts and/or made a purchase to add similar products they may also be interested in (the "customer monetization" stage).

You should have enough traffic driven at every stage of your funnel so that the pixel is seasoned, and therefore you can maximize the key performance indicators for your entire funnel, while increasing the ROI from ad spend. Dynamic Product Ads (DPAs) are essential at this stage of the funnel, so make sure that product feed is set up with Facebook. This includes product IDs, product names, descriptions, price points, and images. These need to be properly uploaded in order to have the DPAs be as effective as possible.

In my company, we typically drive a lot of traffic to the various stages, then focus on DPAs. In my experience, the initial ad should have a certain level of conversion already in order for the dynamic product ads to really shift them into high gear. And in fact, now DPAs have started allowing us to target cold audiences, and this feature has worked really well too. I would recommend testing it to see if it works for you as well.

In summary, the primary concerns with dynamic product ads are 1) that you have enough traffic driven to each stage of your funnel, and 2) that the pixel is seasoned.

Budget Allocation for Each Stage of the Funnel

When we work with clients, if it's a brand new project or they've never driven traffic, most of our focus goes to the top of the funnel. Essentially, it means that the top of the funnel will have a trickle-down effect, and we retarget at every stage.

To evaluate the efficacy of your efforts at driving traffic, you need to look at your cost per click and cost per acquisition (or conversion) for cold traffic vs. warm traffic (or new audiences vs. retargeted traffic).

For a new campaign, we typically allocate approximately 30% of the budget to retargeting and 70% to cold traffic. As the campaign matures, and as we get more leads and warm traffic, that ratio might shift.

It all depends on what the client's goals are. If, say, we are continuously scaling, the typical percentages may not be the best fit. For example, let's say we started a campaign with $3,000 per month, are currently at 50K, and want to reach to 100K. In order to reach these goals, there has to be new blood coming into the funnel all the time. So in this case, we have to increase the monthly expenditure in order to keep the "faucet" on at the top of the funnel all the time, but we can vary the budget based on a) the size of the audience at any given moment, and b) where you're seeing the most ROI for your advertising efforts.

One point of distinction – when we are talking about awareness ads (or branding ads), which involve driving traffic to a content page (a blog, a video, etc.), and then retargeting them, we use what we call "key levels."

Level 1 (equivalent to the top of funnel) is the branding awareness. We set a target CPA (cost per action) on this level (for example, let's say £40 pounds). Then we retarget them.

Level 2 (middle of funnel) consists of anyone who visited the site and/or engaged with the marketing assets, whether it was with a video, a blog post, or the page. We retarget them as well.

By retargeting each time, we have conversion at both Level 1 and Level 2. The converted customers are then directed to Level 3 (bottom of funnel).

Each level comes with its own CPA acquisition goal. So for example, at the lowest level – Level 3 – our CPA has to be less than £6. At Level 2, we are aiming for less than £24. At Level 1, we're looking for £40 or less.

The idea of a successful Level 1 conversion cost would involve people reading the blog post or watch the video and then immediately buying the product. That typically doesn't happen, so we go into that level expecting to barely hit the CPA. However, much better cost per acquisition at Levels 2 and 3 offset the break-even (or loss) at Level 1. For example, for a recent customer, the Level 2 conversion costs ended up being £6 (instead of the anticipated £14), and at Level 3, we ended up paying £4 (instead of the expected £6). As a rule, your Facebook ad account is extremely profitable because the CPA is much lower down the funnel than it is at the top of the funnel. So we typically allocate 40% to 50% of the budget to the top, approximately 30% to the middle, and around 20% to the bottom.

There is, of course, some flexibility built into these figures. If, for example, we have an offer that's targeted exclusively towards the existing customer base, then we might spend a little bit more for that particular week or month.

In an effective Facebook advertising account, budget allocation is relatively fluid by design. In fact, we don't like to stick to strict allocation percentages, and we don't worry about the occasional month where advertising costs end up being a bit higher than usual. Instead, we gauge our progress via two or three KPIs (key performance indicators) for most of our clients. The first KPI is cost per click, the second is cost per lead, and the third is cost per acquisition.

Since there are different CPAs for different levels, we focus our attention on hitting our KPIs, then increase or decrease the budget accordingly (although, obviously, we cap the total spending for each project based on the customer's overall budget).

So for example, let's say you decided to spend $6,000 per month, which breaks down to approximately $200 a day. Depending on the project's needs, you could then spend, say, $100 on Level 1, $50 on Level 2, and another $50 on Level 3. Or you can shift the percentages as needed to meet the project's progress measurements. The most important thing is to keep a close eye on your progress towards the account's CPA and KPI goals.

In our case, after running multiple types of campaigns for a variety of businesses that have both physical and online products, we know what kinds of results we can expect across the board, based on our clients' averages. We set our goals based on those numbers, as well as the current client's profit margins and maximum allowable cost per acquisition.

For instance, one of our clients, a company called Paint Your Life, has an average transaction value of about $300, with the client making approximately $150 in profit. The client allowed us to spend up to $150 on cost per acquisition overall.

Generally speaking, we want to stay below the client's threshold (which, in this case, is $150). So we allocate approximately $100 per conversion from cold traffic, and aim to spend less than $50 for retargeting and converting the existing audience. This is how we calculate the absolute bottom line, provided this allows us to reach the KPIs set for the client.

However, this process is, as mentioned, fluid, and the numbers rarely work out that perfectly. Which, again, is why setting goals around KPIs is so important. There are times when we might need to spend $150, or even $175 in order to make certain campaigns successful. That's okay – just keep in mind that this is all part of the scaling process, and these are temporary conditions that will eventually settle. In the meantime, these bumps in cost per acquisition over the course of a few days or weeks translate into a lot more volume, which makes the extra expenditure worthwhile. Because of this, I'm willing to occasionally break my own rules in terms of CPA, as long as it's a short-term overage (one that doesn't last for weeks or months) that won't end up ruining the overall ROI.

CURRENT FACEBOOK AD TRENDS: WHAT NOT TO DO

Even though this section's title is specific to Facebook ads, the most important advice I can give you is, don't rely on just one channel (including Facebook Ads). As my marketing mentor Dan Kennedy always says, "One of anything is bad!" Limiting yourself to only one big client or a single source for traffic is putting yourself in a precarious position – the old adage about not putting all your eggs in a single basket is an often-repeated cliché for a reason.

Don't get me wrong – I'm a big fan of Facebook. It provides a massive, 2.2 billion-strong active monthly user base, and I would be the first to say that there's no better platform – especially for small business – than Facebook.

But once you reach a certain point, you are going to need to expand. And if you're relying exclusively on Facebook, you run the risk that Facebook might change its algorithm tomorrow, which (depending on the change) could have a very negative impact on your business. I'm not trying to scare you off; I'm just pointing out the reality of how things work in the digital space. Having been in this space for a decade, I can tell you with absolute certainty: things change.

So my first recommendation is to start by getting *really* good at one platform: figure out all your numbers, work out your CPAs and KPIs, and examine the efficiency of your funnel, website, and sales process. Then, using this knowledge as a benchmark, explore other traffic sources.

My second recommendation is to change how you tackle the conversion problem. The average customer is getting savvier every day. So instead of selling, selling, selling all the time, figure out how you can solve your customers' problem. Start thinking about how you can reach them in a way that they don't find intrusive; that they actually love. If they don't like your approach, or your product or service, they're not going to buy.

Note that I'm talking specifically about the desirability of products here – if you're working with commodities, none of this applies because that race is won by whoever offers cheaper, better, and faster.

But if you have a product – especially something that has an aspirational component, that's a little bit high-end – you want to make sure that you're addressing a pain point versus just "selling" to them.

So, to sum up:

1. Don't focus exclusively on a single channel, and
2. Focus on creating a subtler, more appealing approach (rather than just selling more by any means necessary) for your product, and make sure that you're solving the customer's problem with it.

THE (NEAR) FUTURE OF MESSENGER AND CHATBOTS

Facebook Messenger and chatbots are definitely here to stay, but I predict that Facebook will be making regular (and possibly sweeping) changes in how they're used. Since advertising was first introduced to the platform around 2009/2010, Facebook has done an exceptional job in terms of improving the platform for advertisers while still keeping itself and its content relevant for its end users.

Take, for example, the recent algorithm change. I actually experienced it on a personal level approximately three weeks ago, when I started seeing the same posts over and over again. This is a new(ish) development as the algorithm's ability to predict users' interests improves – if the ad is engaging and relevant to a segment of users, Facebook's recently-upgraded algorithm will show the ad to them repeatedly, because the more times an interested person sees that ad, the more likely he is to take action. So far, this seems to be working.

On a global level, this tells you that Facebook has kept their user base largely engaged and strives to continuously improve their platform. I expect the chat platform will get better and better as well – something to look forward to in 2019 and beyond.

TOP 4 STRATEGIES FOR E-COMMERCE OWNERS IN 2019 AND BEYOND

Strategy #1

I look at Facebook advertising as a set of frameworks. So my first recommendation is that everyone should have a clearly defined Level 1, Level 2, and Level 3. You want to constantly scale your ad accounts using brand awareness campaigns, consisting of bringing qualified traffic to your blog posts or contests – any kind of lead generation or free lead magnets you have going on.

Strategy #2

Second, target that cold audience (the people who have never visited your website or engaged with any of the marketing assets you have) effectively with direct response ads (i.e. ads that have some kind of offer or discount, something that asks them to take action right then and there). Make sure to use a variety of formats: posts, videos, images, headlines, descriptions, targeting, etc. You don't want to rely on just one thing.

We've had quite a few clients who came to us and said, "Oh, you know, we tried using Facebook ads, but it didn't work out." The reason for this becomes clear when we dig a little deeper. When we ask them what parameters they tested, what they were offering, how they targeted customers, etc., it often turns out that they launched a single ad campaign, and it didn't work. Which isn't surprising – unless they just stumbled into having the exact right post, headline, landing page copy, etc. all at the same time, the chance of a single ad being immediately successful is extremely small.

We don't rely on that, and we don't think anyone else should either. Instead, you should make sure to have all possible permutations and combinations tested to figure out which ones are most successful for your business. Then keep testing with each new component you add to your mix.

Strategy #3

Retargeting (with either regular retargeting methods or dynamic product ads).

Strategy #4

I highly recommend scaling with the manual bid. There are two basic ways to scale: vertically and horizontally.

Vertical scaling is when you take the ad sets that are already working really well, and then continuously increasing their budget (let's say by 20% to 30%) to expand their reach.

Horizontal scaling involves duplicating multiple ad sets. Again, you take the best-performing ad sets – the ones where all the KPIs are matching or exceeding their goals at all funnel levels – and create multiple versions of it. But here's the key, the secret sauce that really takes it to the next level: when you duplicate an ad, select manual (not automatic) bidding, then use a bid management tool like Companion Labs or Leadza to replicate those manual bids multiple times (thereby turning the manual process into an automatic one).

This gives you the best of both worlds – the ease of automation, coupled with the benefits of manual bidding. With manual bidding, you're able to generate more traffic because you're telling Facebook that you can afford more per click and per acquisition. But with software like Companion Labs or Leadza, you're actually still using automatic bidding, since this software automatically manages it for you.

They also provide a system that ranks all of your ad sets. Based on the cost per acquisition (or cost per lead, depending on what your metrics are) you set, their system gives each ad set a performance grade from A to F. The ad sets with the best performance (i.e. lowest CPAs/CPLs) get an A or B grade; those that are failing get a D or F. So you can literally turn ad sets on and off, but now you just replicated, let's say, a $1,500 ad set into another $1,500 ad set, and then you keep doing that.

One of the biggest advantages of using this automated software for the manual bid is how quickly it allows you to scale your business (provided that you use a campaign that's already doing well – it won't work unless the campaign itself is successful).

BUDGETING FOR CONTENT GENERATION

Most clients and advertisers are primarily concerned with making sales as quickly as possible, and many might have reservations about investing part of their budget into creating content. That's certainly understandable, but potentially shortsighted. If you're selling a commodity product that people already know about and/or already want to buy, and they're just looking for the best price, then you could probably get away with not investing in additional content creation.

However, if you're selling any other type of product, creating a place for potential customers to learn a little bit more about it, showing them how it solves their problem – it's essential. Unless you're a content creation expert, you may have to make an investment on the front end in order to bring in an audience. And while you probably won't see immediate sales from this process, you'll be creating engaging, compelling content that will increase your customer base and yield a better result overall. In other words, it generally pays for itself in the end. If you have bad or insufficient content, on the other hand, you're potentially losing customer interest (and, therefore, sales). For my money, the cost of wasted opportunity far exceeds the upfront content generation costs.

At the end of the day, you should only care about content promotion if it's working. Sometimes it does; sometimes it doesn't. Because the results aren't always predictable, it's very important to test your Facebook Ads mix with and without content at Level 1. The way to gauge content promotion's effectiveness is to look at two KPIs – the amount of time it takes for a prospect to become a customer, and whether the CPA is decreasing. These KPIs need to be monitored continuously to get a clear picture of what is working and what isn't (especially if you're driving traffic from multiple channels, so that you can track attribution correctly).

For example, let's take my company's client, Paint Your Life, again. We tried a content promotion campaign that yielded terrible results. The client bought radio ads as well as spots on Pandora and Spotify, which made sense given the product's universal applicability – the target audience for oil paintings of, say, wedding portraits or pictures of a beloved pet is pretty broad.

We tried the Level 1 and Level 2 approach; unfortunately, they didn't really convert, so cost per acquisition ended up being much higher. But what we also found was that, because we were driving traffic from multiple channels, there was some crossover (for example, someone heard the ad on Pandora, but became a customer via YouTube, Google, Pinterest, Facebook, or Twitter), and we were seeing a cost per acquisition on all those channels. So we were still on the fence about this particular content piece, until we checked the KPIs across the board and found that they were awful.

On the other hand, for another of our clients, a company called The New You, Level 1, Level 2, and Level 3 all work perfectly. In fact, the only way they can increase their audience is by doing Level 1, because Level 2 and Level 3, they don't buy directly.

So, at the end of the day, you have to test all the options and see which one works. And, to me, the winner is whichever offers the lowest CPA and the best ROI.

POSSIBILITY OF CURRENT STRATEGIES BECOMING STALE IN THE NEAR FUTURE

Obviously, video will be around for a long time – I can't see people getting sick of watching videos. I also believe the fundaments – Levels 1-3, dynamic product ads, and scaling with automated software – are essential building blocks of an advertising strategy that will be viable for the foreseeable future.

The only one I'm concerned about is, as I mentioned, chatbots. They're trendy now, and I think they will remain that way for a while, at least (definitely the next couple of years, anyway). But after that, I think they'll start falling out of favor, as people get sick of seeing them in their Messenger feeds. Once that happens, those people will start ignoring those messages, just like what happens with email now. So we'll need to find new and better communication channels to be even more effective (which Facebook will, no doubt, have come up with by then).

*Do you want to see how we have a 1500+ Return on Adspend in a competitive E-Commerce market? You can learn how to get back $15 for every $1 spend on Facebook Ads by going to **www.cvoaccel.com/success.***

CHAPTER 5

Jeremy Howie: The Enlightened Marketing Expert

My name is Jeremy Howie, and I'm the CEO of Enlightened Marketing LLC. Facebook marketing is my thing, with a special emphasis on e-commerce.

I didn't plan to pursue this path originally. I've lived in northern Colorado my whole life, and after graduating from Colorado State University, I joined a landscape design build maintenance company, where I worked for the next 15 years. Although I enjoyed the job itself, I hated the lifestyle I ended up living while working there. I routinely worked 80-100 hours a week, and was always really stressed. Over time, I became very unhealthy mentally, physically, and spiritually, and eventually began drinking heavily and taking pills to face the day.

One day, during the course of a conversation, a customer asked me what my passions were. Although this is a pretty normal question, I was stunned to realize I didn't have an answer. That day, I realized it was time to make a change.

I left the job I had grown to hate, got involved in network marketing and affiliate marketing, then transitioned to video search engine optimization, found Facebook, and the rest is kind of history.

The road to where I am now was fairly bumpy at the beginning. While I was figuring it all out, I ended up having to drain my life savings and my IRAs, but eventually, I ended up getting my first client. However, just as my professional life finally started getting on track, my personal life went right off the rails. Shortly after I took on that first client, I got a call telling me that my brother had committed suicide. A year and a half later, my dad passed away, and a year after that, my marriage ended.

Throughout all of this, I did the only thing I could do – I put my head down, and focused on moving my business forward, providing value, and helping others be successful. This turned out to be the right choice – eventually, I regained my equilibrium, and also found the right track for myself. Today, I'm really focused on Facebook e-commerce. I was invited to join Facebook's SMB counsel, which was really exciting. I've visited Facebook headquarters, I got to meet Sheryl Sandberg, and I've been fortunate enough to be able to provide feedback to Facebook on behalf of the small and medium business communities.

So while it was rough for a while, everything seems to have settled into a good place. As we all know, life occasionally throws roadblocks – sometimes very difficult, painful roadblocks – in your way. The only option is to have faith, and even though it's uncomfortable, to push forward and find a way to make it work.

CURRENT FACEBOOK TRENDS FOR E-COMMERCE COMPANIES SELLING PRODUCTS

Facebook recently underwent a pretty big algorithm shift. Granted, there have been incremental shifts happening for a long time, but this recent one was bigger and more sweeping, reevaluating Facebook's policies in order to improve the user experience.

For example, in the last year, Facebook started cracking down on share-baiting. We stopped being able to include "Tag a friend or comment below" in our content. This change didn't only affect paid ads; it affected organic page posts as well. People who were spending a lot of money on Facebook ads got their ad accounts disabled for share-baits.

So the algorithm keeps shifting, and will no doubt continue to do so for the foreseeable future. As a result, what's working right now might not be working as well by, say, the end of 2019.

Bearing that in mind, the current Big Three Trends are video ads, Facebook Live, and Messenger.

Video ads are working extremely well right now. To take full advantage of this medium, run a video, and then run it again with different ad objectives (e.g. getting some engagement and post-page engagement; getting more consumption of videos with retargeting video views, and then getting some conversions and doing your testing at the conversion base level).

Facebook Live is still ramping up, but Facebook's pushing it pretty heavily, so look for it to become a very big deal in the near future.

And, of course, Messenger's come on strong as well, which I'll talk about in more detail later.

MAKING THE MOST OF FACEBOOK LIVE

Facebook Live has been working especially well for my clients and me lately. You can maximize the results by doing a, well, *live* Facebook Live (so that your page gets the organic Facebook Live), then leveraging the content (going into your ads manager and then retargeting your website visitors over the last 180 days with that same Facebook Live).

For example, let's say you have a clothing brand and a potential customer clicked one of your ads a month ago, but wasn't ready to buy then. That person can be retargeted with a Facebook Live (in the form of, say, a fashion show featuring models wearing your brand's clothes) a month later.

Think of Facebook Live in the same way as you do dynamic product ads. If you're an e-commerce brand and you're not running dynamic product ads, you're leaving a lot of money on the table. All you need to do to take advantage of this option is to create an ad set and campaign that automatically retargets people based on products they've clicked on in the past. At minimum, you should set up Facebook Live based on the same principle.

Beyond that, how you use Facebook Live depends on whether you're a drop-shipper or an actual brand.

If you're an actual brand, the most important idea to take into account when it comes to Facebook Live is that customers want to know that there's an actual person, story, and cause behind a brand. So use Facebook Live to get out there and tell them who you are! Tell your story, tell the brand's story, and show them what separates you from your competition. If you have a charitable component, talk about that. Let them know that, when they buy from you, they're not just Buyer Number 5,012 – they're actually part of something bigger.

If you're a drop-shipping company, your strategy is a little different. Since the recent algorithm shift, video ads aren't as effective as they used to be. Over the course of the history of Facebook advertising, we went from text-only ads to image ads to video ads, and we're now entering the era of live ads. With this in mind, instead of doing video ads, you can run those same video ads as Facebook Lives, and then promote them.

Or you can use Wirecast (or the live video streaming production tool of your choice) to create a new Facebook Live that talks about the product you're selling and/or have models showcasing and using the product, giving the potential purchaser a sense of what it's like in real life.

By doing this, you're going to get a much higher reach, and you're going to see your conversions increase.

FUTURE FACEBOOK TRENDS

As the algorithm shifts, we're going to see Facebook continue to evolve, and to force a good user experience. As marketers continue to try to game the system, we're going to see Facebook ratcheting up its efforts to force brands and businesses to provide value and to use attraction marketing. We've already seen this in action when Facebook shifted away from click-bait or share-bait, and made a push for fewer ads in lieu of more posts from friends.

All of which makes sense, because Facebook marketing – or any kind of marketing, even SEO – boils down to user experience. If you provide a good user experience for your avatar, if you can make them feel good, if you provide them with value and entertainment, you're going to do well on Facebook.

That's basically what Facebook's doing – they're forcing the spam out. So if that's what Facebook's goals are for these recent algorithm shifts – forcing more posts from family and friends because that's what the users wanted – think about what people are looking for in those posts from family and friends, and then make sure you're doing that in your page posts and ads. You'll blend right in!

FACEBOOK ADVERTISING "DON'TS" FOR E-COMMERCE COMPANIES

The big one, which I mentioned earlier, is to stop using click-bait and share-bait. Companies need to get away from saying, "Share this post with your friends" or "Tag a friend that would like this" or "Comment below" because Facebook's really cracking down on that.

Instead, focus on making people want to click and share without being asked, because the value and content you're providing is worth sharing. Make it apply. A good way to do this is to start your post with a question. Let's go back to the fashion brand example from earlier – if you're selling women's clothing, you can start the post off with, "Would you wear this?" You could add a link to that product in the description, or you could just include it in your dynamic product ads or your retargeting. Ask a question, leave it open-ended (i.e. don't make it a yes-or-no question), and get people to comment of their own accord.

Aside from getting away from click-baiting and share-baiting, you should also avoid spamming, as well as targeting the wrong people. The reasons for avoiding spamming are obvious. The dangers of targeting the wrong people are a bit subtler and more complex – in addition to wasting time and effort, targeting the wrong people will cause you to get low relevance scores, which means your ad's going to be shown to fewer people, and you'll get higher CPAs.

To sum up, the general rule of thumb is: don't do anything that will diminish the user experience.

FACEBOOK MESSENGER

Over the past year or so, we've seen a huge explosion with Messenger marketing. Messenger's popularity among advertisers is understandable, given its 90% open rates and 60% click rates, etc. However, the danger here is that marketers are going to quickly oversaturate the medium, just like they did with the News Feed. As a result, Facebook is going to have to put more safeguards and restrictions in place. In fact, they've already started – recently, they changed the Messenger policy to no longer allow discount coupons. I'm still seeing brands get away with that, but it's against the rules now, so I imagine you're going to see Facebook start weeding out the rule-breakers any time now.

My recommendation is, if you're doing anything that's prohibited by Facebook policy, stop immediately. I can see how some people might be tempted to risk it because, for now at least, it still works, and a lot of brands (especially those that are new or don't have a lot of knowledge) are so focused on getting the immediate sale that they'll do *anything* that works.

However, this isn't a sound strategy, because it doesn't take into account the long-term relationship that you're building with a client. You may be going for a $50 sale (with, say, a $20 profit after cost of goods and all your expenses), but it's important to remember that this customer is potentially worth *thousands* of dollars over the course of the next five years, if you play your cards right and you develop a good relationship with that buyer. Using spammy or marginal techniques to acquire a quick sale may be good for immediate revenue, but if you factor in the long-term value of the brand, it's a poor choice. We saw this exact thing happen when email marketing became really big years ago – people got opted into lists, which was okay at first, but eventually it began to feel spammy. At that point, people stopped opening these e-mails, and set up their autoresponders to ding these messages whenever they occurred. If we're not careful, the same thing could easily happen with Messenger.

As with Facebook Live (and any other advertising medium, really), your best bet is to think about how you use Messenger right now, organically, as a person. You're messaging with your significant other or your kids or friends, right? Think about why you're on Messenger versus text or email. Then, mimic that behavior in your advertising. Think about how your avatar's most likely using Messenger, and mimic that. You want to stay within those guidelines as much as possible, because if you're outside of that, you're outside of user experience, and you're eventually going to get penalized. Also, you risk alienating the very people you want to attract.

It's much better to give users the chance to self-direct their experience. You can let people opt-in to Messenger for updates or shipping notifications on, say, the checkout pages. Letting them make a conscious choice (as opposed to having it forced upon them) will engender goodwill, and give them another reason to choose to engage with you. Plus, when you give them the choice and they choose to opt-in, you know these are people who really want to be there and really want to get your content and updates.

You can also retarget people based on that (although, again, no discount codes in Messenger), in addition to dynamic product ads and cart abandonment retargeting.

Another powerful way to use Messenger is to focus on buyers. You can build some pretty good lists on Messenger with buyers only, and while you can't send them coupon codes, you *can* mention big upcoming sales events to a list of previous buyers.

However you choose to incorporate it, keep in mind that, first and foremost,

Messenger is meant to be for content distribution. If you align your approach with user experience and what people are doing organically, you'll be golden.

FUTURE DEVELOPMENTS IN FACEBOOK ADVERTISING

Obviously, we're going to continue to see algorithm updates that will force good/valuable marketing techniques, while weeding out the "bottom feeders." These updates will invariably eliminate spam, and likely lead to an increase in cost per click/cost per acquisition because there will be increased competition for less available advertising space.

As this becomes the norm, lookalike audiences will become an even more important component in marketing strategy than they are now. Lookalike audiences help ensure that you're getting your ad in front of the right people, so Facebook's going to be more likely to give you those few spots. If you take, say, a list of 1,000 existing buyers, create a 1% lookalike from it, and put your content and your ads in front of that 1% lookalike group, you're going to get really high relevance scores, and it's going to secure you a place in the News Feed. So using lookalikes is going to start to push out interest-based targeting more and more.

Facebook is already starting to cut out certain ways of targeting people by interests or behaviors or employers, so you're really going to have to use your existing buyers, existing email lists, and existing website visitors to create those lookalikes to get your ads in front of people. I've seen CPAs for a lot of my clients increase significantly just since the Zuckerberg announcement of the big algorithm update in January. The best way to avoid that is with proper targeting, which results in higher relevance scores, lower costs per acquisition, and a secured spot in the feed.

I also always recommend that e-commerce brands take a hands-on approach to checking out their competition. Visit your top three competitors and click on their ads, their pages, and their websites, so that you get retargeted. Then, over the next weeks, scroll through your News Feed, mobile, and desktop, and see what the competition is doing. Out of every 20 posts, what is the ratio of formats used? Are they Facebook Lives? Are they mostly shared content? Do they use static ads, dynamic ads, etc., and if so, when and how often? You can really get a sense of what's happening.

ADAPTING TO ALL THESE CHANGES AND MAXIMIZING ROI

The best way to protect yourself from the constant changes is, again, to concentrate on providing the best possible user experience. Use high-quality videos and high-quality images. Also, make sure that your ads, content, and images are all optimized for mobile.

Now, when you target someone, target them on mobile; when you retarget someone, retarget them on all platforms: Facebook, mobile, desktop, right column, etc. The reasoning here is, you get the original click or lead on mobile because it's the most cost-effective option (regardless of whether or not they buy or opt in on that original click). However, if you get back in front of them with a retargeting ad, you want to make sure you're reaching them wherever they are, whether that's Instagram, Facebook, Facebook Audience Network (Facebook's partner networks of apps), or anywhere else. Hence the rule of thumb: target mobile, retarget all platforms.

And then, of course, the things we've already discussed are relevant here as well: use Facebook Live and video, focus on user experience, use lookalike audience targeting, and don't use click- and share-bait.

TOP 3 FACEBOOK TIPS FOR E-COMMERCE

Tip #1 is, again, to use video and Facebook Live on mobile for targeting. Getting a video in front of someone on a first touch is going to be much better than a text or an image ad.

Tell your story on the front end, talk about your brand, and show your products in use. Don't try to sell your product on that first touch, or offer a sale – that's like asking for sex on the first date! The goal is to start to develop a relationship with this audience, and like any relationship, that's much easier to accomplish if you start by telling them a bit about yourself first.

Tip #2 is proper targeting. The proper use of lookalike audiences is key, especially if you're just getting started. If you're a new e-commerce brand, you may not have a lot of buyers, or a lot of subscribers to an email list, or even a lot of clicks to your website yet. But what's really cool – and this may be the best Golden Nugget for someone new – is how quickly using lookalike audiences can help you expand your customer base.

One of the ways you can create lookalike audiences is from your video viewers. If you put your brand message out there on Facebook, and you get someone who watches 95% of that video, you can create a lookalike audience based off the 95% video viewer. Later, you can put your more sales-based ads in front of the 1% lookalike video viewers with confidence, knowing that you're appealing to an already-engaged demographic that's going to be much more likely to buy. And again, this leads to higher relevance scores, lower cost per clicks, and lower CAC / CPA.

Tip #3 is the most important of all, and something I've already touched on a couple of times: good user experience and attraction marketing always win the day.

Really think about who your avatar is, provide them with value, address their pain points, and solve their problems with your products. If you look at the direction Facebook is heading in, it's pretty clear that their priority is user experience. Facebook's not going anywhere – they're going to continue to be an advertising juggernaut for the foreseeable future. They're not going to get rid of advertisers altogether (it's a profitable revenue stream for them, after all), but they *are* going to tighten the reins. They listen to their users, and based on that user feedback, they're going to continue to cut out advertisers as necessary.

So do whatever you can to really align with user experience, with Facebook's user experience goals and attraction marketing.

FINAL THOUGHTS

In the near future, we're going to continue seeing paradigm shifts and new tools – that's a given. Pretty soon, I imagine virtual reality and artificial intelligence-based media will get added, and will probably eventually edge out the current best-practice choices. But even as the media formats change, the underlying structure and goals will remain the same. Video, Live targeting, and user experience value is going to continue to be relevant. As long as you're providing the right type of content, targeting the right people with that content, and providing a valuable experience, you'll be successful no matter what happens.

*Do you want to see how we have a 1500+ Return on Adspend in a competitive E-Commerce market? You can learn how to get back $15 for every $1 spend on Facebook Ads by going to **www.cvoaccel.com/success.***

CHAPTER 6

Jeremy Wainwright: Growth Hacker

I'm Jeremy Wainwright, and I've been a Facebook Affiliate Marketer for over 9 years.

I first became involved in digital marketing while I was in college, when I came across an internet ad for an ebook that explained how to make money with Google. I paid $100 for this seven- or eight-page ebook, which turned out to be worthless – someone made money off of it, but it definitely wasn't me! But now that the possibility had been brought to my attention, I decided to see if I could do something with it. I started researching ways that I could actually make money off of the internet. After a lengthy trip down the Google rabbit hole, I eventually found ClickBank. I joined, and quickly earned $100.

After that, I was just hooked. I immersed myself in this new endeavor – it basically took over my life. So began a winding and sometimes-bumpy journey, filled with complications, great ideas, horrible ideas, lots of learning and lots of laughs. From ClickBank, I went on to running pay-per-call offers (before pay-per-call offers became a "thing"). Then I transitioned into supplements and did some local and regional marketing. Currently, I focus on e-commerce – I white-label products and then sell them in my own stores.

It's been a great experience – the internet is amazing, and I love it!

CURRENT TRENDS IN FACEBOOK ADVERTISING: DIFFERENTIATING YOURSELF FROM THE COMPETITION IN 2019

For e-commerce companies, this is a particularly interesting moment in the history of Facebook advertising. A lot of people have been doing things the old way: you send someone to a Facebook ad, they click on the Facebook ad, and they buy your product.

However, as of 2018, Facebook is aggressively transitioning away from that paradigm, and into a relationship-based model. As a result, it's becoming increasingly important to tell your brand story and to put a face (the owner's or an influencer's) on the brand. People need to understand who you are, what you stand for, and what your products are.

A lot of companies are missing that integral first step, and so aren't forming the same connection with their customers. They don't have that lifetime value, and ultimately end up losing money when they shouldn't be.

E-commerce company owners typically fall into two basic categories: goal-oriented and lifestyle-oriented.

The first kind contains people who have very clear goals (either in terms of revenue or in terms of how many people they want to reach), and work tirelessly to create their brand. When these types of owners start scaling up, they sometimes leave behind all of those little customer-oriented services that made them successful in the first place, because the increased sales volume makes it difficult (and often more expensive) to add the same kind of personal touch.

This can be a problem if the reason that their customers liked them in the first place was because they offered those above-and-beyond extras: spending time answering questions on Facebook Live, talking to their customers, writing individual handwritten notes to thank the customers after every sale, or whatever other additional services they provided. For these owners, the biggest potential roadblock is time. When you sell 10 products a day, it's easy enough to provide a personalized experience for each customer; when you sell 1,000 products a day, it becomes a lot harder.

But as your company expands, it's even more important to make sure that you keep those little things, even if you have to change them a bit. I don't necessarily advocate tricking customers, but if a note looks like it's handwritten, that's infinitely better than if it doesn't look like it's handwritten.

And maybe you can't call every customer like you did before, but you should still call some of them. E-commerce is one of those arenas where you have to not only care about your customers, but you have to *show them* you care. Once you lose the customers' belief that you care about them, it's really hard to get it back.

The second type of e-commerce company owners are people who want to live a specific lifestyle (which often includes moving away from being the face of the company) while basically letting their business run on its own. While this is possible, it's really hard to have a relationship with a customer if your business doesn't have some sort of face.

I definitely understand – the attraction of this type of business model is undeniable. There's this idea – or maybe more of a myth – of the self-sustaining e-commerce business, which is so perfectly encapsulated in that iconic image that sometimes pops up on your Facebook: a guy sitting on the beach under an umbrella, getting a tan with his laptop by his side. It's a concept with a lot of appeal, but it almost never works out like that (plus, you'd get sand in your laptop, and who wants that?).

Again, it's theoretically *possible*, but if you want to stay competitive in the market and in e-commerce, the only way to ensure that it keeps going if you're not around is to have amazing people with amazing systems in place before you decide to walk away (then keep your fingers crossed as you go).

WHAT E-COMMERCE COMPANIES NEED TO KNOW IN ORDER TO REALLY BUILD THEIR BUSINESS

The biggest complication that I run into with clients is that everyone thinks that traffic is the answer, when traffic is actually a very small part of the entire equation. Obviously, you should hire an agency (we're all amazing!), but traffic is like gasoline for a fire – it's only able to feed the flames if you already have a fire lit; if you don't, no amount of gasoline is going to be able to light one for you on its own. In other words, traffic is only useful if you have something compelling to direct it to.

This means that you have to make sure that you are very solid on the basics. You need to understand copywriting, know which images create the emotional response you want, have an email sequence, follow up, understand retargeting in traffic sources and in your email list (which entails setting up triggers for specific actions, so if someone hasn't opened any emails, you know what to do; if someone opens all of the emails but never buys, you know what to do, etc.).

Also – and this is a huge one that no one ever does – spend more time with your customer service team. Find out what they're getting asked most often, and then answer those questions in your advertising! Answer them in your emails! People will tell you what they want you to say, if you ask them.

Not only does this improve your customer response; it lets the people who work in your customer service department understand that they ultimately drive decisions, which will make them feel amazing. That's how you retain people – make sure that they know the value of the job they're doing for you, and that you value them for doing it.

Another thing worth noting (and this is a big one): everyone thinks that they need to be everywhere (and, ideally, eventually, you should be). However, to hit that first $10 (or $20 or $50 or $100) million mark, you really only need to get one traffic source right. In fact, your best bet to get there as quickly as possible is to focus on a single traffic source.

You have to create content specific to that traffic source, and upload tons of it, frequently. If that traffic source is Facebook, you need to shoot images that do well on Facebook. If that source is YouTube, you need to create a lot of videos, along with a few hundred bumpers. As we all know, the most important part of the video on YouTube is the first three or four seconds, and you need good bumpers to make sure that, as people are flipping through the channel, they see something that makes them stop. Dive headfirst into one traffic source, and grow your success from there.

Instead, a lot of companies try to port content from one social media channel to another, and can't figure out why it doesn't do as well. The reason is that the kinds of images you should use on Facebook are completely different from the kinds of images that work on, for example, the Google Content Network. Trying to use them interchangeably is just not going to work - it's not even worth testing.

OPTIMIZING STRATEGY AROUND THE RECENT CHANGES IN FACEBOOK

In 2018, Facebook explicitly said that it was shifting the focus of the platform back to a more "user-centric" experience. I love when things like this happen in our industry, and everyone kind of freaks out and screams, "Facebook is changing!"

At its core, Facebook has always been pretty much the same. It cares about two things: 1) how much money they're making per CPM and 2) user experience. If people's Facebook feeds were filled with, say, a constant barrage of ads that tell users they're fat and should lose weight, most users probably won't like that, for a variety of reasons. This makes for a bad experience, and bad user experiences lead to users leaving Facebook. Obviously, Facebook doesn't want that. So if a company submits ads that get rejected by Facebook and they don't know why, they might want to examine what message these ads are sending.

You want to make sure that all of your advertising is engaging, and that people want to interact with it. If you do that, the result will be much cheaper advertising that should get favorable results. However, if your advertising is not engaging, if it looks like an advertisement, it's probably not going to do well, and if it does get accepted by Facebook, you're probably going to end up paying more for it.

In my experience with clients, I've found that most of them have this very definite opinion of what their brand is and what strategies will work best for it. Their approaches are usually high-concept, very expensive looking, and a little antiseptic. However, 9 times out of 10, the creative that gets the best response – across the board – is amateur-looking images and video featuring people's faces and the product in the shot. This is almost always received better than super high-quality, polished videos or very nice-looking static images of the product on a table. In order for your ads to do really well, they need to have an authentic quality, to look like one of your friends posting an image on Facebook. If you can do that, it will crush.

Another area where I often see companies go overboard is with discounts. Your company should have a very clear plan for discounts, one that's firmly rooted in logic. It has to be consistent across all platforms: in your emails, in your opt-in, and in your advertising. For instance, if someone ends up Adding to Cart, and you give them a discount, that's fine. However, when it comes to those who don't Add to Cart or aren't going to come back, you probably shouldn't give them discounts, and you should know this from the get-go.

I've seen clients and customers who have just spun out of control with discounts. It ends up costing them a lot of money, and it also devalues the product. People should be buying your product because it's amazing. If you want to incentivize them to come back with a discount, that's fine, but that shouldn't be the only reason they're buying from you. Plus, given the latest changes in Facebook, bombarding customers with discount offers may backfire if it comes across as too "ad-centric."

FACEBOOK MESSENGER AND CHATBOTS IN 2019

Chatbots and Messenger are a great way to increase authenticity. It's also imperative that you incorporate them into your marketing strategy – at this point, it's one of those things that, if you're not doing it, you're behind.

Based on what I've seen, the most successful applications – both inside and outside of the e-commerce space – are in a more quiz-like (multiple-choice-like or "either/or" questions) conversational format, rather than a more open-ended dialogue.

That said, there's no need to get hung up over what questions to include or the direction that you want to take with bots. The easiest (and probably most useful) answer is always with customer service: go through the questions that people are already asking, and set up your bots to answer them on Messenger. It will save you time and money, and also help with sales since you can explain the problem to your customer better than they can explain it themselves, which is how you get a sale.

I know some people are worried about adding chatbots; that in some circles, there's a kind of stigma of inauthenticity attached to them. But ultimately, as you scale, you're just not going to have enough time to talk to everyone individually, and that's something that everyone understands. We all deal with a phone tree when we call the bank or the electric company, and it's a normal and accepted practice. This is the exact same thing. All you're trying to do is segment people into different groups so that you can better manage them.

Chatbots are also great for automating follow-up, which is otherwise incredibly time-consuming. In fact, the amount of time required to follow up with customers individually is one of the reasons that a lot of e-commerce companies focus very heavily on the first sale, but not really on the subsequent ones. Chatbots in Messenger are a great way to remind people, for example, that if they bought a 30-day supply of a consumable 25 days ago, it's time to order again. As a bonus, this type of follow-up isn't perceived as invasive, and open rates on them are crazy-high.

Ultimately, chatbots are just another vehicle to build a relationship with your customers. As long as you make sure that your bots are set up to have a give-and-take-type conversation with the customer (rather than aggressively pursuing a sale), chatbots can be a huge help to your business.

FACEBOOK ADVERTISING IN THE NEAR FUTURE

Again, Facebook has been clear about returning to a "user-first" model. So, it stands to reason that companies that have a content-first strategy will have the best results on the platform.

A great way to get into content-first is to go through influencers. I've seen a lot of very strong e-commerce companies reach out to influencers to get the content they need for advertising, especially those that sell, say, wearables. The influencer wearing the product in their daily life becomes a piece of content. This kind of content is not only visually appealing, but also attractively simple – it's just a person wearing the product. It doesn't feel like a heavy-handed direct sell, and so those end up doing really well too.

In my own business, I've found that more and more of the advertising that I do on Facebook is outside of the News Feed. Since late 2017, there's been a gradual shift happening towards Instagram, Audience Network, and Messenger. I imagine that as 2019 goes on, we'll continue to see that. All of those other placements that were once thought to be low quality and/or not good for driving traffic are becoming increasingly important in my advertising strategies for my clients.

The easiest way to incorporate these other placements is through retargeting. Facebook has an amazing – maybe even scary – amount of information about each of its users. When you give Facebook the option to use all of its resources, to grab someone via Audience Network or Messenger, and you're optimizing for something like a conversion or a checkout, Facebook will deliver that at the cheapest price across all of the platforms. When you limit Facebook to just News Feed, it's probably going to end up being more expensive.

Plus, if you group everything together, you're going to get more volume; depending on your goals, that can sometimes be even more important than return on investment. For example, for those of my clients who are more interested in getting the entire market than a specific ROI, this grouping option has been pivotal in making sure they get what they want.

ADAPTING, MAINTAINING AND INCREASING PERFORMANCE IN E-COMMERCE COMPANIES

If you have an e-commerce company, marketing for your business will always be your responsibility. Even if you hire someone else to handle the day-to-day aspects, it's still up to you to stay on top of what's happening in the industry, and to make sure that everything stays on track. So you need to make a point of keeping up to date – reading the blogs, showing up at the conventions, and having real conversations with people who are doing this every day. This isn't a particularly secretive field, which is fortunate, since the mechanics change so rapidly that exchanging information is vital. So if you ask people what they're doing, they'll probably be happy to tell you all about it. In my case, nothing I do is super private or proprietary, and I adjust strategies all the time. The reality is that if I'm doing the same things that I was doing 6 months ago, then I wouldn't be good at my job. Every day is about constantly testing and learning, and losing and (occasionally) winning, and then testing some more. That's just how the game works.

TOP 3 STRATEGIES FOR E-COMMERCE COMPANIES IN 2019 AND BEYOND

Strategy #1: One of my favorite exercises to do with new clients is to ask them who they think their customers are, and then look at Audience Insights to see who their customers actually are. Generally, I find that clients think their customers skew 10-15 years younger than they actually do.

Everyone forgets that the fastest-growing demographic on Facebook right now is 65+. Which, depending on your product, might be good news – older demographics tend to have more expendable income. Besides, even if you think that your audience should be 25, that's probably not where you're going to make money – that's a hard market to crack. So it's a good idea to let go of who you think your customer is, use the data Facebook provides to figure out who your audience *actually* is, and tailor your approach to them.

Strategy #2: In an earlier section, we talked about how e-commerce companies need to generate tons and tons of content that's relevant to their audience. Again, this is important for two reasons: first, because Facebook is going to love it, and second, because you can retarget everyone who engages via posts on your Instagram. Since you're dealing with people who are already digesting your content, this has the potential to be a very successful strategy. Generally, these can be a different group of people than those who visit your store or are on your email list. So not only are they a great audience to market to (since they already love your content), they're a *unique* audience too!

Strategy #3(a): Traditionally in advertising, everything was heavily segmented, and marketers chose their target audience via rigid demographic data. However, at this point, the machine does such a great job that we don't have to figure out who to target – Facebook et al. handle it for us. Instead, you can simply run lookalikes off of every existing group: people who bought your product, people who bought your product three times, people who have taken the upsell, people who've opted in to your email list, etc.

Strategy #3(b): After you have all of the successful lookalikes, don't be afraid to run to really broad audiences. I think that everyone has this idea of what their perfect-size audience is – somewhere between half a million and two million people. That's fine, as far as it goes, but don't be afraid of that 10-million-person or 20-million-person audience once Facebook has a decent amount of data.

Keep in mind that, at its core, Facebook is like a very smart baby. You just have to teach the baby exactly what you want it to give you. So after Facebook has seen a conversion ten thousand times, it gets a very clear idea of the types of customers that it wants you to deliver. Once it has that amount of information, you can end up building those bigger audiences. The return on investment in the larger audience is never going to be as good, but that's not the goal here –

the goal is to move the volume. This giant audience is going to spend a ton of money and break even, and then your smaller lookalike audiences are going to boost your ROI.

The most expensive type of customer to get to make a purchase is the cold customer; anyone who has touched you before will be cheaper. So it's worth going after all of these people: the small targeted group, the lookalike audiences, and the larger audiences.

Strategy #3(c): The other important point to remember is lifetime value. Worry less about how much a single click is going to cost for a given person; pay more attention to how much their lifetime value will be. The reality is that Facebook is an auction, and the reason lifetime value is so important is that it gives you more power in the auction when you are bidding against other companies. The company that can afford to spend the most on a click or a customer wins.

So you need to be clear on 1) what your lifetime value is, and 2) how much you're willing to spend to acquire that customer. The more you're willing and able to spend to acquire that customer, the better off you will be.

*Do you want to see how we have a 1500+ Return on Adspend in a competitive E-Commerce market? You can learn how to get back $15 for every $1 spend on Facebook Ads by going to **www.cvoaccel.com/success.***

CHAPTER 7

Mari Connor: Business Strategist Extraordinaire

My name is Mari Connor, and I'm the Owner & Marketing Director at Marigold Marketing Group, an online advertising agency dedicated to creating, running, and managing successful Facebook Ad campaigns since 2012.

FACEBOOK ADVERTISING TRENDS FOR E-COMMERCE IN 2019

A few months ago, Facebook announced its intention to shift the platform back to a "user-first" philosophy. Subsequently, e-commerce companies who want to continue to see success on Facebook need to adapt their own business models accordingly. The best (and easiest) way for them to accomplish this is to invest in a content-first strategy, and focus on community building, rather than on making a quick sale.

Facebook is penalizing brands that don't comply with the new policies by giving them decreased (or zero) News Feed real estate. In order to remain competitive within the market, e-commerce companies should shift their focus to telling stories, creating content that's educational and/or informative, and offering helpful videos that solve their ideal customers' pain points.

Companies that don't make this change, that make (or continue to make) all their content about themselves/their products, will find themselves either becoming increasingly less relevant, or needing to invest more to maintain a foothold on the platform. In either case, it's likely that their competitors who spend time creating content and building communities and lists of avid fans will win (and probably rather sooner than later).

So, if e-commerce companies want to take the easier path to succeeding on Facebook, they need to invest in a content strategy that matches what the demographic is looking for. If they make a continuous effort to create content that their target audiences like, they create a brand with staying power, that can weather the fluctuations in Facebook policy and in the market. What this is telling fly-by-night marketers – business people who want to just come in for the kill, make a little bit of money and get out – is, why not consider building an actual business, and have it feed you and yours for years to come?

The way you do this is by creating content that engages your audience. Often, it's as simple as answering the questions you get asked most often. Every business in America – every business around the world – should be keeping track of the top 10 questions or objections they've heard in the last 6 months in their business, and then creating a Facebook post to answer each of them, with a direct answer and/or helpful information about that topic.

Better still, they could create 10 blog posts on their websites: first, a headline that provides a little snippet of (or an attention-grabbing teaser to) the solution, followed by an entire blog post explaining the answer.

And even better still, create 10 videos addressing those 10 questions and objections.

This is an easy way to start interacting with your audience, and by focusing on the most frequently asked questions you've heard from your community in the last 6 months, you're ensuring that the content is timely as well as engaging.

The best place to incorporate this type of content is at the top of the funnel, to get more people into your community. The ideal audience for this comes from either cold traffic that has peeked at your product, or from the overall demographic that you typically target. Ideally, the titles of your posts or blogs or videos will draw these people in, and the content will solve a problem for them. Then you can make the pitch or do the close a bit later down the line.

A STEP-BY-STEP GUIDE TO CREATING THIS FACEBOOK ADVERTISING FUNNEL

Assuming that you have a website, or somewhere else for this community to go (if not, creating that would be the first step), the first step is to set up a space for blogs on that site. Starting a blog section on your website is probably one of the simplest ways to begin creating communities with your prospects.

The next step is to create those 10 pieces of content described above, preferably in your voice. Actually outline the question and answer as if you were having a conversation with a potential customer, not only providing a solution but also explaining why you do it that way, what variables you take into consideration, and anything else the customer would need to know about the topic. You might want to hire a VA who specializes in editing this kind of thing to edit it down.

Next, create a Facebook page. If you're selling products that fit the same demographic, try to create a page that's inspiring to that demographic. For example, for women, that concept could be living your best life with your family, and you can create a Facebook page revolving around that inspirational idea, catering to that demographic. It can be called by the brand name, if the brand name alludes to what you do; if not, maybe choose something that's in keeping with the theme of the page. Then start posting your blog onto that Facebook page so that you're sending traffic to your websites. Install a Facebook pixel on your website (it's not difficult, and you can find instructions on Google) to track your traffic.

The reason that I believe that blogs are so important is that they've proven themselves to be an incredible resource. We track our clients' data, and when purchases come in, we can track them back to where they originated. Over the last 75 or so clients that we've worked with, we've found that in general, there have been 5 audiences that proved to be the most successful, and which need to be built continuously:

1. The first (and most profitable) audience is website traffic, and the easiest way to build that is with your blog.

2. Video viewers. In order to keep these people engaged, you need to regularly create videos on Facebook.

3. The email list. Two or three years ago, uploading this with the Facebook ad tool would have yielded the highest sales. Today, however, we're seeing that blog visitors and video viewers are both purchasing more than the audience from the corresponding email list.

4. Page engagers – people who are engaging with your page, which needs specific memes to be targeted to the appropriate audience.

5. Your Facebook fans. A lot of Facebook specialists debate whether or not it's worth growing the number of likes on your page or the number of fans. I'm a firm believer, because I've seen that it can be monetized. I've had clients say, "Well, we've heard that likes are only for vanity," to which I reply that if I couldn't monetize them, I wouldn't recommend it. However, since I *can* monetize them, I want to grow them. I treat them like another mail list – I want to make sure that each fan routinely gets some of our posts and some of our blogs to keep them warm, just like an email list.

So, to sum up: write up those 10 blogs, upload them to your website in a blog section, and then start running them to your likely traffic, specifically the traffic that's most likely to purchase your product long term. Once they've gone to the blog and read it, they'll get pixeled; you can then retarget that pixel traffic for a purchase.

E-COMMERCE "DON'TS" FOR 2019

The main practice I would advise against is using in-your-face "sales-y" or "promotional" tactics and copy. Facebook has made it clear (and their policies confirm) that they want ad copy to look like a social post, as if it came from a regular Facebook user. So be careful with caps, emojis, etc.

Also, if Facebook tells you that your ads have too many emojis or too many caps, or that the colors in your images are too loud or a little too bright, or whatever (sometimes they'll give you this information; sometimes they don't tell you anything, and simply disapprove the ad), bear in mind that whatever standards and practices Facebook has in place, chances are good that other platforms are going to follow soon. So if this is an issue that keeps coming up for you, it might be a good time to re-think how you create ads.

In general, try to avoid anything that might read too "advertise-y". Maybe have someone in your target market take a look at it – sometimes we can't tell how our copy comes across to others, or we're so proud of what we do that we just assume everybody's going to like what we created too. When you start running ads, you'll start seeing who's clicking, and which blog post seems to be attracting the most audience members. The results are often surprising – it can be hard to predict what will capture your audience's attention, and it's frequently not what you would expect.

I recently experienced this phenomenon with a painting contractor client. We posted blogs on a variety of topics in that field. I expected the audience to want to know more about the materials they used or what the top paint colors will be for 2018 or something like that, but it turned out that they loved the blog post that explained how contractors break down their pricing (which I never would have guessed). As a result, we're creating more sub-blogs on that topic, because the market has told us that this is the content it wants.

FACEBOOK MESSENGER AND CHATBOTS IN 2019

Before incorporating the latest trends into our business model, we like to watch what's going on in the market; over time, the direction these trends are likely to take becomes clear. Like lead ads – I see fewer and fewer lead ads in my News Feed lately. Now, this might be because, when someone opts into a lead ad, they have to do so little work that the lead quality is lower, or it might be for some completely other reason entirely. The important part is that, for whatever reason, the market is pivoting away from leads ads (at least for the time being).

Similarly, when a new tool is released, we prefer to adopt a wait-and-see policy – we want to see how it ends up working in the marketplace. So far, overall, I think that chatbots are extraordinarily useful tools, and that Messenger bots can be useful as well. However, the minute that they start to feel like you're chatting with a bot – reminiscent of the auto-attendants in corporate phone trees, you know: "Press 1 for X, press 2 for Y, press 3 for Z," etc. – they start to become annoying (or, worse, off-putting), making the user feel that he won't be able to get a real answer here. It's important to watch out for that when incorporating a bot.

For getting people engaged, or maybe answering a couple of their initial questions, fine. But I wouldn't recommend trying to program the bot in a way that's meant to trick users into thinking they're interacting with a human, because a) it's unlikely to work, and b) users will experience that annoying, frustrating feeling that they're not going to be able to accomplish what they want to accomplish there.

For instance, a lot of people set up Messenger bots to follow up on the initial contact with yes-or-no questions. But sometimes the answers are "maybe"; sometimes they're gray areas. And in those moments, users can be left with the impression that this brand doesn't care about customers; they're just trying to box you into an oversimplified, black-and-white sort of response.

In my opinion, chatbots are more effective when used in a less involved way, for example when running an ad that asks the user to reply with a brief response (e.g. "I'm in!") to an event invitation or about a new product, and then sends them the link to, say, the event or product page (which is bound to have a more human voice), from which they can then contact the company, or whatever they need to do.

My company uses chatbots in this very limited kind of way: giving the user a word or short phrase to type into the interface in order to send them some additional information, or even to send them the link to an actual landing page opt-in form.

The other reason we limit our use of chatbots like this is that we're big believers in the idea that, just like with lead ads, if it's too easy opt-in, you risk ending up with a lower-quality list. You want just enough friction that people need to stop what they're doing to type in their name and email address, because just that little bit of friction tells you they're serious about wanting the information.

The research data confirms this phenomenon. When online influencers did a comparison study by sending traffic directly to a lead ad (where the customer only had to click once or twice) vs. sending them to a landing page, they found that long-term sales were actually higher when the group went to the landing page. The obvious conclusion is that this small amount of extra effort is just enough to ensure that you're attracting the right people to your list.

I have personally had better luck just creating blog posts related to the products and their peripheral topics (like in the paint contracting company I mentioned earlier). Maybe it's because I often end up focusing on more intricate topics within the industries that I'm trying to advertise (so the questions/issues that are being addressed appeal to a concentration of people who are more deeply involved in that industry), but I've found that I'm able to build an even higher quality audience by just having them visit the page and then retargeting that for whatever we need.

With that being said, I'm sure there are people out there who have a lot of success with lead ads or with ManyChat. I've always been a big fan of the idea that, if something's working, by all means – continue to do it! If you've found some pattern or some strategy within your business that more in-depth use of chatbots or lead ads accomplish, that's great! No two businesses are exactly alike, and the testing (and testing and testing some more) process is important for this very reason!

ADAPTING AND MAINTAINING/INCREASING PERFORMANCE IN 2019

As the audience becomes increasingly sophisticated, they also become increasingly more disenchanted with any approach that feels artificial or glib. As such, I think the most important thing a business can do throughout 2019 is to adjust its overall tone and copy (both on its site and in any advertising and promotional materials) to make itself seem as honest, human, and *real* as possible. Get in the habit of writing the same way that you speak, using the same words and phrasing that you'd typically use in your daily life. If you take a step back and give your more promotional or "sales-y" ads a critical once-over, more often than not, you'll come away from them thinking, "Who talks like that? I don't sound like that when I'm in my store (or online or when I'm on the phone with a client or with a prospect)!"

Chances are, when you communicate with someone in real life, you use subtler, less pointed (or blatantly manipulative) language, and probably answer questions simply and directly. Which makes sense – I think most people would prefer to have a friendly conversation with someone, rather than feeling like they're constantly being prodded towards something.

It's an easy mistake for advertisers to make, as these are the kinds of ads we all grew up seeing and hearing. Sometimes, when I watch TV or when I listen to the radio, I feel like I'm hearing ads that I see written on Facebook. The problem is, the protocols don't translate – approaches that work in a TV ad don't necessarily work in a more casual, communication-centric platform like Facebook. I've encountered this with a lot of businesses – I can tell from their copy that they're writing what they feel should be in a radio or TV ad, and I just want to tell them, "Stop that, and go back to telling stories!"

Speaking of which, another thing that businesses could start doing – and I know this is a huge ask because I recommend it all the time, but I rarely see businesses take the initiative – is to come up with one story from or about your business every day. Did someone with, say, a serious condition come in, and your product helped? Did your product solve someone's problem? Did it make someone feel amazing? Help make someone's day better? Being able to tell that story (with or without mentioning their names – if you don't feel comfortable giving out clients' or prospects' names, you can just say something like, "This woman, [age], came in today, here was her issue, and here's how we made it better") makes for much more genuine and engaging advertising, which is exactly what you want for this medium.

Recently, I was consulting with the owner of a small dress store here in Scottsdale, and I recommended that she adopt this strategy for her social media – to tell stories about the women that came in, and she made a very good, very universal point that I think is true of pretty much every business owner on the platform. She said, "That's all I do! I talk to the visitors who come into the store all day, every day. I have thousands of stories I could tell!" To which I responded, "Then in the name of all that is holy, please start documenting them!"

If you have a store and have interacted with customers who are happy with their purchases, the stories become even more powerful if you get them involved directly. Get them on the phone or record a video interview with them – anything you can do to showcase testimonials from people who are fans of your business and products. You can do this regardless of the type of store you have (whether brick-and-mortar or online-only e-commerce) – just tell the customer something like, "If you wouldn't mind, I'd love to get you on camera. This way, you can tell other people about how you use this product and what it did for you."

OTHER TRENDS DEVELOPING GOING INTO 2019

First and foremost is video. People should be paying more attention to videos, and finding ways to engage their audience with video.

I also love the new Watch feature on Facebook, both from a personal and a professional standpoint. On the personal front, Facebook Watch has been reminding me about episodes I've missed from influencers I like to follow, including some of my favorite late-night talk show hosts who have already signed up for the Watch feature. I found myself binging on several episodes in a row.

Facebook seems to be promoting this quite heavily – they've added a unique notification on users' home pages and phones to alert them immediately whenever a new episode is released, and some businesses are doing a good job of taking advantage of that now. It's what's trending at the moment, and doing double-duty by getting the masses accustomed to making and consuming video in much larger quantities on the Facebook platform.

Which brings me to why I love Facebook Watch in a professional capacity – it creates a very accessible way to build the five crucial audiences I mentioned earlier, in a manner that is comfortable and engaging for them.

TOP 3 STRATEGIES FOR 2019

#1: The first and most important strategy is building those five audiences (website visitors, video viewers, your email list, your page engagers, and your Facebook fans) I talked about previously.

Build the website visitors group through blog traffic campaigns, the video viewers group with video view campaigns, the email list group with conversion campaigns, the page engagers with post engagement campaigns, and your Facebook fans with a combination of the above. This is the key to moving your business forward.

If you're a brand, it shouldn't take much effort for you to boost ads and get a ton of likes, comments, and shares. Then you can use the ad tool to build an audience of people that have engaged with your content.

As for your Facebook fans, don't be afraid to say, "Hey, like our Facebook page! That's where we post all our most up-to-date information!" I have a client that does tax protestation in Texas, and they add a note and link saying, "Like our Facebook page because this is where you'll get THE up-to-date notices on how to properly file your protests, how to audit them, what the deadlines are, etc." at the end of all their emails.

When new clients come to us now, we basically say, "We're going to set up all the campaigns that we need in order to build those five audiences, because that's where our data has shown that 90%-99% of sales have come from." Plus, I'm a big believer in sales coming from warm audiences in general.

This idea is where I typically get the most resistance, by the way – I get a lot of comments online from e-commerce business owners who say, "I can close cold audiences just fine." Which, again, is amazing, and I firmly believe that if it works for them, they should absolutely continue to focus their energies there. There are always going to be exceptions (which is why it's a 90%-99% rule, because nothing will ever apply 100% of the time). But overall, warm audiences are where both your first sales *and* your long-term sales are going to come from. So if you're serious about building a long-term business, keeping those audiences engaged and growing is Job One.

#2: The second strategy involves taking cold audiences, thoughtfully introducing them to your brand, and holding off on the hard-sell or pitch until the audience is sufficiently warmed up to that brand. You know – let them kind of poke around and see what you're all about first.

#3: And finally, we're making sure to put social proof ads out there whenever and wherever we can. We have clients who run multiple events, so if we're running a campaign that's similar to one we've done in the past for them, we'll reuse the ads that built up social proof during the previous run(s) for the new event.

You can start building social proof by, for example, running a click ad and testing 3-4 audiences, images, and copy. Take whichever one rises to the top in terms of lowest cost or highest return (either one is fine; either will give you an idea of the direction it's going) and put that post, exactly as is, on your page. Then run all your cold traffic to that post, because the social proof will continue to build on it.

*Do you want to see how we have a 1500+ Return on Adspend in a competitive E-Commerce market? You can learn how to get back $15 for every $1 spend on Facebook Ads by going to **www.cvoaccel.com/success.***

CHAPTER 8

Mike Pisciotta: The Marketing Guru

My name is Mike Pisciotta, and I'm an ex-con who spent 10 years in prison, then turned my life around. Now I'm an internet marketing junkie, Facebook Ads fanatic, and I just love everything having to do with e-commerce, online marketing, funnel optimization – just a whole bunch of geeky, nerdy online marketing terms!

These days, a lot of my time is devoted to helping two e-commerce brands with their strategies, especially with all the new things that are happening within the internet marketing space. The rest of my time is spent consulting for companies that are starting to incorporate direct response online marketing components into what they're doing. I also spend a lot of time on Facebook (obviously) just seeing what's working, hanging out, chitchatting, and generally getting a feel for what people want.

I found my way into this industry after I got out of prison. Unfortunately, there aren't a whole lot of opportunities waiting for you when you're an ex-con. Going on a traditional job search didn't work – nobody would hire me. And, since going back to the lifestyle that got me sent to prison in the first place wasn't an option, I had to grind and find work wherever I could.

My very first experience with online marketing involved posting craigslist ads and selling stuff through them. While doing this, I learned a little bit of HTML and started taking on clients. This was back in 2009-2010, when you could still game the craigslist system by, say, hiding nine paragraphs of keywords that nobody could see. We added HTML and used hex code to make the text white so it was invisible, and then we'd stuff all these keywords in there. I had clients that were paying me $100 a week just to post these listings in cities across the country.

This worked for me – I enjoyed the challenge of this process, and decided to branch out a little. I started learning how to write copy, I started learning marketing, I invested in programs, and figured it out as I went along. I found I had a knack for it, and eventually this morphed into a career. My wife and I went from doing craigslist ads and then Facebook ads (the kind that existed way back when you could only run ads in the right column and there were no other options) to building websites, to providing a full-service internet marketing model. Next, we transitioned to strictly consulting, teaching, and training. Then about three years ago, we dove headfirst into e-commerce, and decided to tack that on as well.

FACEBOOK ADVERTISING TRENDS OF 2019

Facebook Messenger is what's happening right now. This is where the attention is, and I see it as a retro throwback to when AOL and Instant Messenger were the order of the day. I remember when email was just the coolest thing ever, when you'd hear the famous "You've got mail" announcement from your AOL account and get super excited about it. That's what Messenger is like right now. Messenger is how people are communicating with their friends and families. And brands that understand that, that are becoming part of the conversation, are crushing it. I'm using it across my e-commerce brands and in information marketing spaces. We've been doing some cool stuff with Messenger for a few select clients, and the results have been really exciting. We've seen 98% open rates and 50%, 60%, sometimes 70% click-through rates on Messenger. It's been a big hit with early adopters. I think the results will be even more impressive when Messenger is coupled with some other new tools and features that Facebook has released recently.

For example, there's now a split test option at the campaign level, which is something that I'm been trying out. I'm excited about the possibility that this can help address audience overlap, an issue that has caused a sharp spike in our cost per acquisition over the past year or so.

Now, there have been some creative ways to kind of get around this issue, but once you get to the point where you've reached millions of people with your ads, audience overlap is pretty challenging to break through without some really unique configurations, especially if you want to go broad. So it's exciting that Facebook is starting to roll out some options that can help address this. Split testing at a campaign level allows advertisers to get past the overlap and avoid creating marketing fatigue.

At the moment, Facebook offers split testing for delivery optimization if you want to optimize for conversions or impressions, and also for placements and audiences. Previously, if you wanted to run a split test, you had to kind of set it up manually. The introduction of the new feature makes it possible to split test on a much larger and more precise scale, which allows us to really harness the power of the Facebook algorithm.

Plus, as a bonus, Facebook receives the data from the split tests as well. This is great because the more data we give them, the more they're going to be able to optimize; the more they optimize, the better the ad delivery system; the better the delivery system, the better your results.

WHAT COMPANIES CAN DO TO ADAPT TO WHAT'S HAPPENING IN FACEBOOK

Where I find companies are falling short is getting up to speed on all the new changes happening in Facebook. The game has changed completely in the last few months, but these companies are trying to market in 2018 like it's still 2016 or 2017.

There's so much competition in the News Feed, there are so many advertisers trying to get out there, and costs are rising. We can either succumb to the whole Chicken Little syndrome – we can gripe, we can moan, we can get tear our hair out and scream, "Everything's imploding!" – or we can just be better marketers. We can figure out creative ways to bring in new customers, to use the tools and features Facebook has released in a way that will allow us to run Facebook advertising profitably. Sure, the landscape is completely different than it was in 2016 or 2017, but there's no reason why you can't still make it work for you.

One of the things I've started doing that I never would have before 2019 is using automatic placements. A year ago, it just didn't work – instead, I would choose between News Feed only, desktop, mobile, or some combination of them, and I did Instagram placement in completely separate ad sets.

Now, though, I'm finding that the algorithm has improved tremendously, and Facebook can really pinpoint where a user is likely to convert or click with far greater precision than before. This is a perfect example of what I was talking about in terms of avoiding the mindset of, "This is what worked in 2017 so I'm going to keep doing it." If I had clung to my previous habits and perceptions, I would never have been able to reap the benefits of this new capability that Facebook has developed.

You have to reevaluate old strategies. Try out new features, and take another look at options that you may have put aside in the past. This is a time and place where companies can really start gaining advantages by bringing updated features and new ideas into their marketing mix.

WHY THE DIZZYING ARRAY OF EXPANDED OPTIONS FOR ADVERTISERS?

Why is Facebook suddenly focusing so much attention on providing new tools and placements for advertisers? The answer is very simple, and exactly what you would expect: money.

At the end of the day, Facebook is like any other business – they wanting to grow, and for that to happen, they need a constant influx of users, advertisers, and dollars. Facebook needs to hold on to their advertisers just like they need to keep their users. To that end, they're constantly coming up with ways to get us to stay.

So if ads in the News Feed have reached the saturation point, Facebook has two options to keep revenue going: they can either jack up their prices, or open more locations to ads. If they jack up their prices, it'll just make people angry, and cause them to migrate back to Google, which offers lower costs. Facebook's much better off saying, "Well, if the News Feed is jammed, what we need is more space to offer to marketers."

Obviously, Facebook is opting for the latter. You can now run ads in the marketplace, in Messenger Home, in-stream videos, and in Rewarded Videos.

I predict that, by the end of 2019, Facebook will start to allow ads inside of groups – they've tested this, and they've seen a positive result.

It's an interesting balancing act for Facebook, because they can't just create a new placement – they have to acclimate users to the idea before they just start placing ads wherever. People need to get used to interacting with the platform in a new way in order for it to become a successful venue for advertisers to run ads.

I believe firmly that Facebook makes a real effort to understand its *entire* audience (both users and advertisers). They're really good about taking both perspectives into account when setting their policies. I've worked with Facebook's account managers enough to know that Facebook's goal is to keep marketers on the platform. They want us to stay, which means they want us to get results, so it's to their advantage to create a good advertiser experience as well as a good user experience.

HOW TO CHOOSE AMONG THE NEW OPTIONS ON FACEBOOK

If you're a new e-commerce business, one that hasn't had consistent sales yet, start with a smaller budget. Test a couple of ad sets, and spend your time getting to know your audience. When you have a smaller amount to spend, you have to rely more on your ability to provide quality data to Facebook. In order to be able to do so, spend time understanding who to target, where to place ads, how to appeal to that low-hanging fruit so that Facebook can start getting the data it needs to optimize and to do its job for you.

Also – and again, this is something I wouldn't have advised a year ago – when you're just getting started, you don't have the data for Facebook to optimize your delivery for purchases right out of the gate. So instead, I'd recommend that you start a little bit further back in the funnel. Maybe start by optimizing Add to Cart, since that action happens a lot more frequently than a purchase. Start there and test, and depending on how it goes, maybe move forward.

Even with some of the bigger brands, we're testing InitiateCheckout as an optimization because we're getting that more often than purchases (although a little bit less frequently than Add to Cart), and that's helping to push some of those costs down. The strategy has been successful, and I think starting a little bit further back in the funnel would work well for small businesses too.

If you're brand, *brand* new, start at Page Views and/or Add to Cart, and add some really good retargeting. At the very least, you're getting traffic to the site and building a targeted audience. Let the retargeting do the heavy lifting. A year or two ago, we relied on cold ads to do all the heavy lifting for us. Now, due to the increased competition, things are changing, and retargeting is going to cost you a lot less.

If, on the other hand, you have an established brand, you've been around, you've got thousands and thousands of purchases, obviously lookalike audiences are going to work better for you, together with some very segmented retargeting.

The smaller-business strategy mentioned above could also work equally well for you, just on a larger scale and with a bigger budget. Try optimizing with the InitiateCheckout pixel event: allocate $200, $300, $400 (or whatever your budget allows) per day to this event.

Your goal is to get those folks to take action – to add something to the cart, maybe go through the checkout process – and then we can do some retargeting. The retargeting effort should be product-based, collection-based, and specific to the user. You don't want to send them a generic, "Hey, come back, here's 10% off" message; no, it needs to be meaningful. Show them a private video and/or some benefits of the product. Get creative. Spend the money to get people into the retargeting audiences, and then do some really cool, powerful segmented retargeting to them.

WHAT E-COMMERCE COMPANIES SHOULD START DOING IN 2019

At this juncture, I think mixing in Messenger is imperative for the success of a business, especially if chatbots are incorporated.

Messenger is already a powerful tool, and it's poised to become more and more essential over time. Companies that take advantage of the power of the algorithm in creative ways are going to start seeing advantages, including a decrease in costs. This is the most important piece of advice I can offer in terms of adapting to the new reality of Facebook – figure out how you can really *use* the data you get from Facebook and the algorithm to find the right people. Messenger is absolutely a large part of that, but so are the tools Facebook offers. You just have to find the combination that works for your particular business. If that means doing automatic placements, great – do that. If you think somebody on Audience Network is going to convert, run with it. If you think having 10 different images is going to be more effective, by all means – have 10 images! Empower the algorithm to do what it does best.

Dynamic Creative ads are a really effective way to provide the algorithm with data. When the algorithm is running and a person has seen the same ad multiple times, it starts to throttle down the impression, because Facebook doesn't want to keep showing the ad to someone who's not going to take action. The Dynamic Creative empowers the algorithm by giving it more options to test the various components of the ads – the headlines, text, buttons, images, etc. – to see which of them are the most effective, and which combinations work best for each audience.

I know it seems counterintuitive to cede so much control over results to an automated system. Again, as recently as six months ago, I rarely used Facebook automated features, preferring to maintain control of the optimization. I did separate desktop and mobile ads, Instagram in a separate ad set, Instagram Stories in another separate ad set, Audience Network by itself, News Feed by itself, right column by itself, etc. It's what I was used to, and what worked.

Over the last 6 months, however, when I tried to take that same approach, my results just tanked. And the times when I basically let Facebook have its way and said, "You know what? Go ahead, I'm going to leave a lot of things set to automatic," my campaigns were more successful. There are, of course, still some elements that I control "manually," but it's probably less than 70% of what it used to be. Facebook's gotten so much better at learning and understanding people in general (and their users specifically) over the last year that we can kind of trust them now. Plus, the tools that Facebook's introducing are designed to empower us to hand over more of the details to them, and get better results because of it.

Again, I think this is especially helpful for somebody who's just getting started, who has less than a thousand purchases from their store. Letting Facebook's algorithm do most of the work, knowing that you can rely on them to get you the results you need – it makes the process much less daunting for someone who's new to it. I'd say that if you have 5,000 or more customers, you could take a little more control of the details, if you feel it would be helpful. However, even in those cases, I've been seeing slightly better results lately when more of the dynamic options were chosen, and the algorithm was given free reign to do its thing.

I also believe companies at that stage – with thousands of customers and thousands of Add to Carts – would benefit from the split test option. It lets you fine-tune the results that Facebook provides, without limiting the algorithm. With the split test option, Facebook itself is using the data it amassed to figure out where to place, where to deliver, and who to deliver to, and you're going to end up seeing better results across the board.

WHAT E-COMMERCE COMPANIES SHOULD STOP DOING IN 2019

First, I've said it before, and I'll say it again – stop approaching Facebook like it's 2017! 2019 is a whole new world, and you need to adapt your strategy to the new reality as quickly as possible.

Second, consumers are a lot more sophisticated now, and if you want to have a chance at appealing to them, you need to develop a profound understanding of how they interact with Facebook.

One of the approaches I've seen work really well is combining ads with Messenger. So instead of having someone click on an ad, a landing page, or a product page, we want to open up conversations. Consumers want to be heard, and they want to interact with your brand. So rather than saying, "Here's my product, go to the page and buy it," you want to try to start a dialogue: "Hey, would you like to learn more about [x]?"

For instance, if you're offering, say, tattoos, you could ask, "Do you want to learn about the various color options available?" Make it so they want to get to know your brand, get them involved in the process – you're not trying to get a one-time purchase; you're building an engaged audience who will buy from you over and over again.

This ties right into the ethos that Facebook has started consciously cultivating since Mark Zuckerberg's January 2018 announcement, when he made it clear that Facebook was going to be re-prioritizing social interaction.

This more social approach is what works now, and what will no doubt continue to work going forward. Besides, honestly, this method feels much more natural than just hammering away at the low-hanging fruit, basically yelling, "Buy my stuff! Buy my stuff!" Instead, we want to get feedback, to really understand what is getting people to engage and interact, and to forge relationships.

FACEBOOK MESSENGER AND CHATBOTS IN 2019

Chatbots are my favorite of the new Facebook tools, and they can be tremendously helpful, but only if you use them correctly. One of the biggest mistakes I've seen: companies who aren't making it clear that the "representative" answering users' questions is actually a bot. This can infuriate users – when people have 4 or 5 engagements with, say, Customer Service before realizing that they haven't been speaking with a real person like they thought they were, they tend to get angry. So if you employ a chatbot for this type of function in your business, it's a good idea to make it very, very clear to the audience that this is what's happening. You can do this by, for example, creating an opening greeting along the lines of, "Hey, you're chatting with XYZ Corp's friendly chatbot! I'm here to help you with your XYZ Corp question."

One of the best things about chatbots is the extent to which you can personalize them. In my own brands, we're adding personality to our bots that reflect the general personality of the brand itself. This works well because Messenger is a very informal platform. It's not like email or a business phone call; it's a much more relaxed atmosphere, which gives us the ability to inject a bit of fun and humor into the format. You can make the interactions really conversational, creating a unique and enjoyable experience for the customer.

When it comes to bots, it's a good idea to give people a good number of options. Unlike in traditional conversion principles, where you take away options if the audience doesn't do what you want them to, Messenger works better with more variation. To make the experience more engaging for your audience, you want to give people a lot of options to choose from. Plus, this gives you the opportunity to tag and segment people based on their responses, which will allow you to achieve better results, period.

An important point to note about advertising on Messenger is that, when someone messages your page and automatically becomes a subscriber, you're only allowed to send them promotional material within the first 24 hours after the initial contact. If that 24-hour window has elapsed, you can no longer send them anything promotional, but you can message them. This gray area is a good place to employ some strategic thinking. If you can't send your subscribers promotional materials anymore, you can send them a blog article, for example, to recapture their interest. Once they reengage, the clock starts again, and you can send them promotional stuff again.

This rule is one of the ways that Facebook makes it really clear that they want marketers to give people something valuable, something that they actually want to interact with (as opposed to a "Hey, once you've got subscribers, spam the hell out of them and keep bombarding them with promos" policy).

It's actually pretty helpful – if we just listen and pay close attention to the terms and rules Facebook puts in place, we'll know exactly what they're looking for from us.

FACEBOOK'S CONTINUING EVOLUTION THROUGH THE YEAR

Throughout the rest of 2019, Facebook's likely to continue to roll out more tools like the split test feature, Facebook Analytics, and Dynamic Creative tools (although probably more granular) that are going to empower marketers to relinquish more and more control to Facebook in order to get better results.

One tool we already know about is the upcoming ability to accept payments right in Messenger. Messenger has already had a feature that allowed users to send money to friends, but there was no "pay for purchases" option, and the function wasn't available via chatbots. Which makes sense – Facebook knew that if they let marketers get into that space right away, people wouldn't use the feature.

So they introduced the "send money to friends" element in order to start acclimating users to the concept. Once people got used to it, Facebook could add the extra components that make it an attractive prospect for advertisers and businesses. Eventually, Facebook's going to find an opportunity to take their own percentage from payments made through Messenger, which is fine – if using a proprietary Facebook payment system decreases some of the friction that could keep a customer from making a purchase, it's completely worth whatever nominal fee they charge.

Beyond that, Facebook's marketplace is going to be really hot for physical product brands. They're working on some really cool ways to deliver better, more robust product recommendations to people in specific areas and topics. So if you're thinking about becoming a brand owner and/or physical product seller, the next 6 months will be the optimal time to jump into the Facebook marketplace, and really get your store positioned to take advantage of what they have to offer.

HOW TO IMPROVE YOUR RETURN ON AD SPEND ON FACEBOOK ADVERTISING IN 2019

There are three keys to adapting to the new Facebook environment, which I've already touched upon:

#1: If you're not on Messenger, get on there. If you don't know what you're going to do with it, just start building a subscriber base, start getting people to interact with and send messages to your page, and gradually, you'll get a sense of what else you can incorporate that would be beneficial for your business.

#2: Relinquish control to the algorithm, and look for creative ways that you and your business can give Facebook the ability to do what it does best.

#3: Reprioritize content. Not too long ago, everything in marketing was "content, content, content." Content was king. Then Facebook became the new hot platform, and we started kind of drifting away from that, because Facebook made it so easy to put your offer in front of the low-hanging fruit.

However, given the direction that Facebook seems to be headed, we're going to be seeing a return to "content first." If you want to attract customers, you'll need to create high-value content, engaging videos, etc. to get people interacting with your brand. If you focus on content and implement tools like Messenger to engage with your audience in 2019, I think you're going to see incredible results.

THREE STRATEGIES TO USE THROUGHOUT 2019

Strategy #1 is to incorporate slideshow into your campaigns – it's a fantastic tool in general, and very effective for e-commerce brands that are just getting started.

When we use slideshow, we set it to optimize for video views, with the goal of getting cold traffic to see our products. There's a maximum of 10 slides per slideshow; we'll usually use between 5 and 10, depending on what we're doing. So with a single ad, we're building an audience of people that have interacted with multiple collections and/or product features.

Then, we can take that audience and retarget them, and build lookalikes from the list. On top of that, Facebook themselves are actually recommending this feature. They said it's working really well, which means they favor advertisers that use it, so you're going to see a lot more impressions for a lower cost.

Strategy #2 is one that we already talked about: start pulling your optimization a little bit further up the funnel (instead of purchases, retarget at Initiate Checkout). This was a strategy that my Direct Facebook Ads account manager recommended to me. Up to that point, we were focused exclusively on Add to Carts and purchases, and occasionally page views. He correctly pointed out that, when looking at our events, there were a lot of Initiate Carts, and if we refocused on those, the algorithm can use that data to deliver our ads better. We tried it, and it ended up working beautifully.

Finally, **Strategy #3** is all about – and I can't stress this enough – Messenger, Messenger, Messenger! No matter where you are in your company's lifecycle, start getting people into Messenger. You can run an optimized ad delivering a freebie, an offer, and/or a good piece of content directly to your audience in Messenger. Also, reduce as much friction as you can – if people send a message, give them the video, download, or e-book right there in Messenger, and let them engage with your content.

Nothing is future-proof, especially with Facebook. The best way to protect yourself and your business from getting blindsided is to have a solid strategy in place, one based on creativity and an understanding of what makes people tick. You can never go wrong by actually caring about your customers (current and prospective) and delivering the kind of value that you know they want.

Get back to basics with a solid, content-centric approach that's designed to make people actually want to interact with your brand and care about what you're putting in front of them. Bring them in, engage with them, provide them with education on the benefits of your product, and show them how it can solve their problems. Make your customers your priority, and I think you're going to get some really impressive results, no matter what the rest of the year – or, for that matter, the future – brings.

> Do you want to see how we have a 1500+ Return on Adspend in a competitive E-Commerce market? You can learn how to get back $15 for every $1 spend on Facebook Ads by going to **www.cvoaccel.com/success.**

CHAPTER 9

Molly Pittman: The Consultant's Consultant

My name is Molly Pittman, and I'm a marketer and educator. My passion is discovering, testing, and figuring out digital marketing strategy, distilling it down to a simple step-by-step process, and then teaching other people how they can implement these new strategies. I love to help people grow their businesses, or to help them grow their clients' businesses.

It's actually kind of shocking that I ended up here. When I started as an intern with a digital marketer, I didn't even own a laptop! I know, right?

I'm originally from Kentucky, where I earned a marketing degree, but had been taught mostly very traditional marketing methods. While I was in college, I had an advisor named Dr. P, a business owner/consultant who taught a few classes. I adored her – she was the reason I became a business major in the first place.

In my senior year, I took a class called Entrepreneurship taught by her. There were only nine of us in the class, and we spent the entire semester building business plans and pitching them to her business investor friends.

At the end of that semester, she took me aside and told me, "Molly, when I was first starting out, I worked at a bourbon distillery called Buffalo Trace. That was really cool, learning traditional marketing, you know, prints ads and stuff that's been around for hundreds of years. I knew going in that that wasn't a forever thing, but it got me started."

Then, she mentioned that she'd just gotten back from a conference in Austin, and said it reminded her of me. She said, "I think that's where you need to be. If you move down there, even if you don't have a job, you'll work it out. That's where the opportunity is for your skill set."

Being from a really small town in Kentucky, I barely even knew where Austin was. But something about it struck a chord with me, and sure enough, two months later, I signed a lease, packed my things, moved to Austin, and started bartending. Soon, I started looking for a job in my field, and stumbled across an internship on Craigslist that asked, "Are you open-minded to learning new things?"

As it happened, yes, I was! Now here I am, five-and-a-half years later, with a career I never could have predicted when I first decided to follow in Mrs. P's footsteps and "go bourbon."

So I think my journey helps me be a better teacher in this space because I know how it feels to be just starting out. And when you can put yourself in the student's shoes, I think that's when you're really able to deliver an effective message.

BECOMING A SUCCESSFUL DIGITAL MARKETER

When I first started checking out job postings on Craigslist, I was looking for a marketing position. I didn't even really think about digital marketing, specifically – my education hadn't touched on this area much. I just felt like, since I had this marketing degree, I should have a marketing job, right?

So falling into digital marketing was kind of a fluke. Really, the Craigslist ad just spoke to me. The copy was, of course, amazing – it basically said, "We own a bunch of companies and are looking for new people who are willing to learn." They were hiring a group of interns for a 3-month internship program, and if all went well, they had a few full-time positions available at the end. They also mentioned that they had drinks at the office and liked to hang out, which was a big selling point for me at the time, so I applied and got the internship.

To my surprise, I discovered that I actually really love this stuff! As soon as I started learning digital marketing and funnels, I knew I'd found my calling. I love people, and marketing is really just understanding people and giving them what they need or want.

I really enjoy what I do. It doesn't feel like a job; it's just who I am. I think if you find a career where you feel that way, you will succeed no matter what because it will never feel like a burden to you. I know most people spend a lot of time searching for that, and I'm lucky to have found it early in life. I've also been lucky enough to be surrounded by really great people. I've had wonderful mentors like Ryan Deiss and the team at Digital Marketer: Richard Lender, Russ Henneberry, Lindsay Martyr – these are my people, and we kind of went on this journey together. Having an amazing team helps you to keep going.

Plus, there are the customers, and teaching, and students – that's really why I do this. I love being able to create or produce a podcast episode and then get a message like, "Molly, I implemented the thing you talked about, and got these amazing results!" I had someone come up to me at TNC a few years ago to tell me that he implemented a Facebook ad strategy that I taught, and it worked out so well, he was able to pay for his daughter's entire college education within a few months. That's hugely rewarding.

So it's a combination of love for the job and, of course, hard work! You have to put in the time and the effort to keep learning, because this stuff changes every day. In the digital marketing field, nothing's ever written in stone. It can't really even be taught in traditional higher education right now because it changes so frequently. Facebook, for instance, changes practically every week!

We have a unique opportunity to really take advantage of this new wave of e-commerce. Recently, I read an article that said that, out of the top 10 most in-demand jobs right now, 5 of them (like, for example, online community managers) didn't exist five years ago! So, there's this unprecedented opportunity to build a career without having to have any formal education, because there really isn't any. All you have to do is just be willing to dive in and try.

FACEBOOK TRENDS IN 2019

I think 2018 is my favorite year so far for Facebook advertising, actually. At the beginning of January, Mark Zuckerberg made this big announcement that the News Feed is changing, which really doesn't change a lot for advertisers necessarily. But what it did do was give us direction.

He came right out and said, "This is what we want the platform to be. We want advertisers that are actually starting meaningful conversations." Which chatbots can facilitate. Which is perfect timing, right? He says that he wants what's best for actual Facebook users, and although he didn't say this directly, my interpretation is that he's saying that user experience is more important than ad revenue.

He realizes that, especially with the recent election and all the associated turmoil, Facebook is one of the most influential platforms – probably the most influential platform – ever seen on planet Earth. It has the power to alter the way people think, and it has to take that responsibility seriously.

From an advertiser standpoint, that means we must put out quality ads. This is stuff that we've been teaching for five years as a kind of "best practice" suggestion, but it's now becoming a requirement. There's no way around it, and I love that, both as a marketer and as a Facebook user.

The hands-down best way to create a quality ad is to have it tell a story. Even if you're selling an e-commerce product that you think is a total commodity, there's still always a story that can be told. And that's what people want to read on Facebook. They don't want to be directly sold to, but they're totally open to checking out new products that are related to them and have a cool story. Brands that have given them value in advance, brands that are starting great conversations on Facebook, utilizing Messenger – these are the companies that people are happy to incorporate into their lives. So that's where I feel we are with Facebook advertising at the moment.

THE IMPORTANCE OF BRANDING

I also believe that branding is more important than ever before. Not that an ugly website can't still convert, but it's going to become more and more difficult. Online consumer behavior is changing. I buy most of my stuff online – even my groceries are ordered through an app. I rarely go into a store anymore. And most people are starting to head in that same direction.

If you think about it, your online store – your online home – is the same as a brick-and-mortar. Would you want to walk into a shady-looking store that isn't welcoming, and makes you question if it's a legitimate business? You might go in there if they have something you really, really need, but it's not a place where you want to spend a lot of time. You want to go into stores that are beautiful, that are open, and that lead you through them; stores that make it clear that they value your business.

The same thing applies to online businesses, especially e-commerce. And I believe that, in 2019, you're going to continue to see that. For e-commerce, branding the way you look and the experience you're providing to users on your site has never been more important, because if you don't provide it, they'll go to a competitor who will.

There's also a huge emphasis being placed on trust, especially for Millennials. They don't just want a company to have appealing products; they want to shop at companies with which they can align. They pay attention to what the company stands for, and whether it's making shopping a fun experience for them.

Allbirds, a shoe company (and one of my favorite brands right now), are a perfect example – they do exactly this. They sell these really cool wool shoes that, while a great product, aren't anything extraordinarily special in and of themselves.

Yet, while I'm not a shoe person, I have six pairs of Allbirds at the moment. Why? Because they're just so good at marketing and telling their story, their site is awesome, their emails are great, their Instagram keeps me engaged; they are a *brand*. They've built this relationship with me, and every time they launch a new color of their shoes, I have to have them!

WHY SOME COMPANIES HAVE SO MUCH TROUBLE TELLING A STORY

It's hard not to live in a direct response mindset when you're building a company, especially an e-comm brand where you have overhead costs and shipping to think about. Plus, you need to be very careful with your margins and your cost for acquisitions. So it's hard to say "I'm going to go invest 15 grand in this beautiful branded website" when you can't necessarily track what that's going to do for your business. And even if you wanted to test a new, wonderfully branded site against your old one, that's still a huge investment to make.

I believe that it's because the market is still lagging a bit. People will probably stay in this mindset for maybe another year, and the year after that, we'll start seeing a bunch of beautifully branded sites. But the people who have already made this switch or are doing so currently are really winning right now. They have all this extra time to leverage the audience, to build relationships and trust with them.

For example, I'm working with a supplement company that sells a daily multivitamin. The product is a supplement that helps regulate your circadian rhythm, which is a huge deal in the health space right now. When I came onboard, they had a single sales page that looked like it was from 2010 – the copy was super long, very direct response. And it's not that it couldn't work – we could probably run traffic to it and sell this supplement, but it wasn't a brand. I said, "Guys let's invest in a really nice site, a really nice brand that people can get behind. Let's create a story around this."

Basically, instead of just saying, "This will help you fight fatigue and make you feel better," we built an amazing site that's about to launch, and renamed the company Rhythm (because that's what it does: it regulates your body's internal clock). The brand's mission is, in part, to educate people about the fact that each body is different – we need different amounts of sleep, we don't all need to eat at the same time, etc. Americans have major fatigue and stress issues, and a lot of that stems from not paying attention to their bodies. So if you want to regulate your internal rhythm, this supplement can help.

Taking a few extra months to build that brand from both a visual and a story standpoint helped us tremendously. It was worth taking that extra time, because now I can run Facebook ads about people's body clocks and their circadian rhythms and how we're going to help regulate that vs. "Here's a free trial of this supplement. It'll make you feel better." Create the story behind it – people want that, they want to build that relationship.

WHAT E-COMMERCE COMPANIES NEED TO DO TO ADAPT IN 2019

The most important thing an e-commerce company can do for itself is to figure out its story. Every brand needs a story that helps to clarify its message. It's also really important to invest in the product, because if your site's awesome but the product it leads to is underwhelming, the customer's going to be disappointed.

While I was doing market research for the supplement company I mentioned, I came across another brand called Ritual. The product is a multivitamin, mostly targeted towards women, in a unique, transparent bottle. They have a beautiful, compelling, and informative site (www.ritual.com) that's absolutely worth a visit.

This type of branding is becoming an expectation across the board. So e-commerce companies should focus on the story (the "why"), and make sure that their sites look as great as their products.

Beyond that, it's obviously also very important to build out great systems for acquisition (whether that's through Facebook Ads, traditional marketing funnels, chatbots, or any combination of platforms), and really think of your business as twofold. You need to be acquiring new blood into your business on a consistent basis at a reasonable price, but you also need to focus on the monetization and reengagement of those people.

I see a lot of companies get stuck in one of those two areas. They want one funnel that's going to acquire all these customers and make a ton of money, but that's not really how humans work online anymore.

Today, it's about using your acquisition funnels, hoping you can break even to acquire these new customers, but also about focusing on, say, communicating with your email list. A lot of business owners, especially of e-commerce companies, forget that they have this whole pile of people that have shown interest in the past. Whether those people actually purchased from you before or not, those are your best people.

So it's really about *focusing* your marketing efforts. Of course we want to bring new blood into the business, but we also want to constantly give value, reengage and further monetize those people with whom we've already established a relationship.

WHAT COMPANIES SHOULD STOP DOING IN 2019

At this point, it's clear that we're pretty much past the point of a purely direct-response marketing strategy. I'm sure there are people still doing it, but it's really, really, really hard to build or even maintain an e-commerce company now that's purely direct response, without a website and a blog and a social media presence. Because in the current environment, if you don't have these things, as far as consumers are concerned, you don't exist. Or, worse yet, you look like you might be a scam.

So saying that you don't want to put money or time into social media or Facebook ads or building bots because you might not see that immediate direct response return on ad spend is really a flawed way of looking at things. Because if you *do* have that monetization part of your business running and you're a solid marketer, even if you have to "go negative" to acquire these customers, it's worth it – those people just need some time to build, and once they do, the process will more than pay for itself.

Going back to Allbirds for a moment – I recently did a Facebook Live event with Ezra Firestone where we talked about Allbirds, because he loves that brand too. As he pointed out, these aren't shoes that either of us *needs*. It's not a category of shoe that could be considered a necessity; it's a cool, fun "extra" that you purchase because it captures your attention.

He mentioned that he'd seen a bunch of their ads and was interested, but didn't buy for 3-4 months. Cut to today, when Ezra's probably bought 20 pairs for himself, his wife, his godchildren, and his business partners – it's become a signature gift that he gives people in his life.

If Allbirds had been planning their marketing from a purely direct-response standpoint, they probably wouldn't have captured him because from a "what's the CPA today, tomorrow, the next day?" standpoint, he wouldn't have seemed like a good prospect to keep reaching out to.

Instead, Allbirds got him because of their willingness to invest in making the market aware of their products, because they know they have a good story and that they can retarget.

A lot of it is also really getting into the mindset of your potential customers. What is the thought process that leads them to buy your product? If your marketing can facilitate that, you're going to win.

For example, your approach needs to reflect the lifecycle of the product you're selling. The amount of time that elapsed between Ezra finding out about Allbirds and buying his first pair is perfectly reasonable for a shoe brand. However, if you're selling toothpaste, you're probably not going to spend 3-4 months warming someone up to your brand. Toothpaste is something that people need in the moment. So if you're present, and have made them aware of your brand, that person will automatically remember you.

Even with those more commodity-type products, you have a chance to tell a story and set yourself apart. Most people selling toothpaste would focus on general product features ("It's whitening! It's fluoride-free!") or generic concerns ("It's cheap! It's good quality!").

But if I'm your potential buyer, I already know all of this and, more importantly, all your competitors are saying the same things. Because it's a commodity product, most marketing is of the "Hey, you already know what toothpaste is – we've got the best price or the best quality, so buy it from us" variety.

If those features are selling points for me, I'm going to compare the components I care about with other toothpaste brands anyway. You'd have a much better chance of convincing me to buy your toothpaste if you run a really funny video ad or talk about how the toothpaste relates to something else that's going in my life, positioning this toothpaste as something I identify with. Even with commodity products, you have a huge opportunity to tell a story and set yourself apart.

Now, while I think it's worth putting money aside to create a story and a beautiful site, you have to make sure that you're not just doing branding for branding's sake. Going back to the toothpaste example, having an ad for Colgate featuring a picture of a tube of toothpaste with the logo across it isn't the type of branding I'm advocating. That ad does feature the word "Colgate" and shows you what Colgate is at its most basic, but it doesn't tell me anything about the brand. It doesn't tell me a story that's going to set Colgate apart.

The kind of branding I'm talking about – good branding – goes a step beyond that. How could Colgate set itself apart from the pack? For starters, they could forego concentrating on toothpaste altogether, and instead focus on my life as a busy professional instead. How can Colgate speak to that and position their toothpaste as the toothpaste for someone like me? Or focus on some other aspect of my life where a smile by Colgate could help the situation.

This can be done in a million different ways. If they wanted to target people who like to travel, they need to answer the question, "Why is your toothpaste great for me when I'm on the road?" and create an ad centered on that.

Basically, great marketing keeps in mind that people are never really buying things or products – they're buying an end result. They're buying an emotional response, or a solution to a problem, or a way to make something in their lives easier. As such, the best branding focuses on the product as a vehicle to a desired outcome or end benefit, rather than on the product itself.

CURRENT TRENDS IN FACEBOOK MESSENGER AND CHATBOTS

When Facebook released Facebook Messenger ads in 2016, it created a need in the marketing community to build bots. Bots had been around before, but once Messenger came onto the scene, people really started to take notice of them. Last year, interest in bots spiked as people started trying to figure out just what the heck they are and how to use them. Most started using Messenger like email, which is *not* a good idea because they're very different platforms.

In 2018, it seems to have normalized, and we're seeing practical application of bots that make sense and are useful. We've reached a point where chatbots are becoming normal.

As marketers, we're learning how to use them, which is great because bots and Messenger marketing are all about being conversational. This is not a one-to-many broadcast like an email ad – it's more akin to receiving a text on your phone.

This is a massive adjustment for marketers, especially in terms of figuring out how to drive traffic into the bots, and what to do once people start engaging with them. Fortunately, consumers are becoming more familiar with bots too. They're starting to see ads in their Facebook Messenger, and are becoming accustomed to getting their shipping information from an e-comm company through Messenger. Basically, as marketers continue to sharpen their skills and consumers become more comfortable with the platform, the next year is shaping up to be huge for Facebook Messenger marketing.

To take full advantage of this new medium, companies have to get into the right mindset. The first thing you need to understand is that it isn't really about building bots. I've seen a lot of people get overwhelmed at the idea because they think that they have to build a little bobble-head representation of their company that answers any questions that a customer might ask. That's totally not the case. The only companies that have bots like that are big brands that have spent hundreds of thousands of dollars to develop them.

At its core, a bot is really just a sequence of messages and technical functionalities, kind of like an email auto-responder. For your purposes, think of this as just another marketing channel, one where it's best to implement a few simple strategies first.

There are some really simple things e-commerce companies can do with these bots, like retarget their custom audiences, or run ads to cold traffic that leverage the click to a Messenger ad inside Facebook. You can link that with the JSON growth tool and ManyChat, and the ad can promise some sort of coupon code. So maybe you're giving 10% or 20% off for new customer acquisition, or to get your warm audiences to buy. You can promise that coupon code in an ad – just set the expectation that it's going to be delivered in Facebook Messenger.

That's a very important thing to keep in mind – wherever you're running traffic from into Messenger, make sure you're always setting the expectation that this is going to happen because it's still very new. People will think it's a bug or something.

So run that ad and/or promise the coupon – they click, they engage with your opt-in message, become a subscriber, get the coupon code, and are sent off to use that coupon code. Now they're subscribers to your bot, and you can add them to a sequence where you can follow up with them to give them more content. You can be promotional within 24 hours of the last time they engaged with you. The opportunities are endless.

Now that ManyChat has a Zapier integration, you can still ask for email and all of the information that you want. And now that ManyChat has rolled out payments inside of Messenger, it makes the entire process seamless. Say you're selling a fishing pole – you can send a discount coupon and a message showing photos and the product description pulled from Shopify, saying, "Hey, do you want this product?" directly to users scrolling through their Messenger feeds. They can click on the product and enter their credit card information, the transaction is processed, and they get a confirmation message. Meanwhile, all the order and shipping details are right there on Facebook. It's such a frictionless process for the end-user!

The same strategy could work for delivering a lead magnet if you're selling an info product or if you're a service-based business. I have a few clients for whom we've simply taken some lead magnet funnels that they've used before, and transitioned them to Messenger. We use the same ads, and just add a little bit of copy about Messenger.

Which is great because we're still delivering the lead magnet, we're still getting that email address, but the customers don't have to go to a landing page. Across the board, everyone's seeing a decrease in opt-in rates because consumers are tired of filling out form fields. It's like going to the doctor and filling out all those intake forms. No one wants to do that anymore; everyone wants the process to be instantaneous. With Messenger, they don't even have to go to your site! Everything happens right there, and then we add the payments. This is the year that Messenger becomes a real commerce platform.

There are also a whole host of new tools, like ShopMessage (www. shopmessage.me), that allow you to implement simple tactics. For example, let's say people visit your Shopify store and look at a dress, but they don't buy. If they're logged into Facebook and they've engaged with you, you can retarget them – as soon as they abandon the cart, you can send them a message that says, "It looks like you forgot this" or "Here's a coupon code" to help overcome the barrier to purchase.

This is a marketing channel, so ultimately, we're going to focus on acquiring subscribers, creating communication plans to give people value, and really make Messenger a place where you're building that relationship. But in the meantime, there are a bunch of little strategies that people can start with, so that they can integrate this new tool into their overall strategy gradually without getting overwhelmed.

THE FUTURE OF FACEBOOK ADVERTISING

Over the course of the next year, I think you're going to see more of the same kinds of things we've been seeing lately. The people that are willing to really tell that story, really give value, make people laugh, and make them cry – the good marketers – are going to keep winning. As long as you place your trust in the idea that building relationships with your audience will, in turn, build your business, and as long as you have great monetization strategies in place, you'll succeed.

I also predict that the paradigm will continue to shift over to Messenger. You're going to see Messenger become a commerce platform. People are going to be able to successfully launch businesses just through Messenger. Not that I think you should have a business that relies exclusively on Messenger – it's never smart to rely on a single traffic source. But it's going to be so easy! I'm not technical in any way, but in 2-3 months, I'll be able to set up a Shopify store, set up a ManyChat account, and acquire customers and monetize them, process payments – basically do everything through ManyChat and Shopify, despite my lack of technical ability.

It's incredible – we're so lucky. Granted, this is simply another channel, and it's still important to build traditional web funnels. But it's wonderful that we have this at our fingertips, and that we're getting to discover it together!

First and foremost, bot building and Messenger marketing is about figuring out a strategy where we can get some traction, and get this tool to work. I think that, by the end of 2019, we're going to see some really out-of-the-box things happening on Messenger, things we haven't been able to do in marketing before.

HOW E-COMMERCE COMPANIES CAN KEEP THEIR FOOTING ON THE CONTINUOUSLY SHIFTING TERRAIN

The two most important things you can do for your company are 1) make a point of educating yourself about changes in the field, and 2) pick a few strategies, implement them, and see if they work for you before trying something else. Don't try to do everything at once. Test a strategy thoroughly before either incorporating it into your overall plan, or discarding it. When you find a strategy that fits your current business and marketing assets, implement it on its own. Then, as you start to get a feel for how the platform works, you can really add on from there.

THREE STRATEGIES E-COMMERCE COMPANIES SHOULD INCORPORATE RIGHT NOW

First, of course, is Messenger marketing! Start off easy. Even if you're just retargeting, say, people who abandon their carts, just do one thing. Start building that Messenger subscriber list, and carve out some time and some resources in your business to test that. Even if you don't get the direct-response-level CPA results you're looking for, you're building a new asset and investing in now.

Second, again, really invest in the branding. Invest in your look and feel. Invest in your reputation. Invest in making a lasting first impression, because that has a huge impact on your business. What do people think when they visit your site? If someone visits your site, are they going to come back? Do they trust you? Were they intrigued by your brand?

Third, tell that story! Quit trying to sell the toothpaste, and sell the end result that people want instead.

*Do you want to see how we have a 1500+ Return on Adspend in a competitive E-Commerce market? You can learn how to get back $15 for every $1 spend on Facebook Ads by going to **www.cvoaccel.com/success.***

CHAPTER 10

Sam Bell: Social Ads Virtuoso

I'm Sam Bell, a digital entrepreneur and media buyer. Since 2009, I've been actively buying media, purchasing ads across multiple channels including Google, Facebook, and a few others as well. So far, I've enjoyed every minute – it's been an awesome ride!

I started my career as an IT administrator for the US Army Corps of Engineers in Atlanta, then transitioned into real estate, where I built a very successful career buying and selling houses. However, even before the 2008 crash, the real estate market in my area had started to slow down. A lot of the people who'd previously purchased properties were no longer buying, and it was becoming unsustainable. I realized that if I wanted to survive the market, I had to figure out a way to attract buyers outside of just my local area. By that time, I had already done some affiliate marketing, and was familiar with SEO. Back then, Facebook was still new, YouTube was *brand* new, and no one had done much with these new technologies yet.

So, hoping it would work, I entered this new world and started leveraging internet marketing to find a broader audience for my properties. I was probably one of the first people to actually record a walk-through of one of my flips and upload it to YouTube. It worked better than I'd expected – the process started generating leads really quickly.

Fast forward to 2007 – I went to a real estate investing conference, and while I was getting to know some of the other attendees, the gentleman who had put on the event overheard me talking about my process, and took an interest in this new-to-the-real-estate-industry approach I was taking. When I told him a little more about it, he asked me to share my story with the other guests.

I put together a 30-minute presentation – content only, no images or anything – and shared what I was doing, how I was using blogs and YouTube to market and generate leads. Afterwards, one of the other attendees, Colin Egbert, approached me and said, "We need to create a product; we need to teach people how to do this!" I thought that was a great idea, and that's exactly what we ended up doing. I was the content creator, he was the sales guy, and long story short, the product ended up doing $2.1 million in sales within the real estate investing niche.

I enjoyed working on this project, and was impressed by the enthusiastic response it received. So, a couple of years later, I launched my own info products, created a software platform for people who wanted to invest in real estate, and started doing coaching and training, all while establishing relationships and contacts within the real estate information marketing community.

In 2009, I decided to leave that business and start my own online ad agency. I'd been considering making this transition for a while, but what really decided it for me was the big Google Slap that took place that year. At the time, Google started banning accounts based on their internal criteria. So all of a sudden, advertisers who had been spending thousands of dollars a month on Google got shut down, and (obviously) were no longer allowed to run any ads. This was a major problem since, at the time, they were really the only game in town – the Facebook platform hadn't yet matured enough to support large-scale advertising, so Google was the only place for information marketers to market and sell their products and services.

By that time, I had figured out how to be very successful with the Google Display Network, so I started doing some consulting just based on the relationships I'd forged. I found that I really enjoyed the technical analysis aspect of the marketing business. After working with a few consulting clients, I decided that this was something I really wanted to do. Shortly thereafter, I started my agency.

ADWORDS VS. FACEBOOK

Facebook does a really good job – I mean a *really* good job – of analyzing exactly who your customer is through the psychographic and demographic data they have at their disposal, which allows you to do targeting with pinpoint accuracy. Google's system is more direct-response oriented, and results depend on which platform you're using. In Google, if you're using a search network, that's more intent-based (since people are actively searching for something specific), whereas Google Display is more direct-response in nature (users aren't looking for anything; they see your banner ad or video, and you're just testing their attention).

My background with both Google and Facebook gave me the opportunity to leverage the two platforms' individual approaches and combine them. By doing so, it became possible to kind of transfer Google's intent orientation into the Facebook platform, resulting in data analysis that had the best of both worlds – demographic and psychographic *and* also based on some identifiable intents as well.

2019 TRENDS IN FACEBOOK ADVERTISING FOR E-COMMERCE COMPANIES

There have been a lot of sweeping changes to Facebook in 2018. At the beginning of the year, Facebook made a statement indicating that they planned to reorient the platform towards content that users want to see. This caused a lot of concern in the advertising community, even though it doesn't really affect advertisers that much.

Really, all it means for most of us is that we need to lead with engagement instead of just trying to sell a product or service directly. It means creating interesting content to engage users and create awareness, then really leveraging your retargeting strategies to bring back those people who actively engaged with the content, and with whom you've already established a relationship.

Additionally, going forward, chatbots are obviously going to be a huge thing; not only do they allow people to directly respond to your advertising, they also give you the ability to really follow up with people and engage them.

Traditionally, this was done through email, but as we all know, email open rates are relatively low, and continue to decrease over time. Chatbots don't have that problem (at least for now), so actually being able to build a list of people with whom you can engage via chatbots is a really big deal.

Then, obviously, videos continue to be a main staple. The direction that video seems to be headed is really interesting, too: now that video is a normal, expected occurrence, Facebook is pushing the envelope and coming out with episodic shows. As a result, we're going to see a lot of people getting into the content creation game in the coming months, building audiences by posting episodes. This would be a much more structured show format than the live streams and one-off videos we're used to; it would entail episodes being released on a regular schedule. While this feature isn't widely available yet, it's going to be a huge trend in the near future.

FACEBOOK ESSENTIALS FOR E-COMMERCE COMPANIES

First and foremost, e-commerce companies need to have very specific, sound video marketing strategies in place, running both video ads and in-stream ads. This should also include a strategic remarketing strategy – how are you going to re-engage those customers?

I find it amazing how many e-comm companies don't really leverage retargeting, when a strategic retargeting plan is such a crucial element of the process. For example, if I'm running an e-commerce store where I have tons of different products that people are going to engage with, I want to implement a dynamic retargeting strategy, where I'm offering additional products to re-engage that customer base. However, if I'm running a specialty store focused on one particular product or a curated set of products, then it would make more sense to go straight into implementing a focused retargeting strategy instead.

So, just to recap: I recommend using dynamic retargeting for covering multiple SKUs at once, then follow that up with focused retargeting of people who show interest in specific products. This combining of strategies can lead to incredible results, especially when you have a big e-commerce business and a solid advertising budget. With this approach, you can use your focused retargeting in a Messenger ad, which creates engagement and generates a better response than a "click here and click there"-type ad.

FACEBOOK "DON'TS" FOR E-COMMERCE COMPANIES

I think that companies should spend much more time doing research. A lot of people in the e-comm world take a kind of "spray-and-pray" approach, where they just throw a bunch of stuff out there and wait to see what works. They don't really take the time to do market research, to see what people are actively buying and what the market wants so that they can create a product assortment strategically.

Also, companies need to stop knocking off what their competitors are doing. There are a lot of copycats in the e-comm world, and while there's nothing wrong with doing competitive research, you want to avoid flat-out copying someone else. Not only is it unethical, but doing so also makes it impossible for you to stand out from the crowd. You're much better off researching what your competition is doing, then seeing how can you improve upon it – how you can differentiate your products even if you're offering something similar and/or how you can improve the customer experience. Even when you're competing with companies that have huge sales figures, it's entirely possible that they have areas of weakness that customers dislike. If you make even a small tweak that addresses one of these issues, you can capture the consumers' attention *and* make yourself stand out within the marketplace.

CHOOSING YOUR PRODUCTS

Amazon is probably your best resource for finding out what people are actively buying at any given time. You can go to Amazon and see which products have tons of reviews and feedback. eBay is another great place to do competitive analysis, and believe it or not, so are TV commercials. I know this is kind of old school, but when you watch commercials, you're benefitting from top-level market research. The big box stores and big brands are spending millions of dollars on advertising, so you know they spent a fortune on research to ensure that they get ROI for those advertising dollars. Also, infomercials – a lot of people ignore them, but you have to bear in mind that companies are spending a lot of money to run those ads.

With TV ads, pay particular attention if you see an ad more than once. Those ads are being run repeatedly because they're making someone a lot of money. And even if it's just a seemingly one-off infomercial product, don't discount it out of hand – you're looking at something that people are actually spending money on, and when you're looking to increase your own sales, it's always a good idea to follow the money!

FACEBOOK MESSENGER AND CHATBOT "DON'TS"

As mentioned previously, chatbots are a great way to engage your audience as well as to create another channel where you can market to them. Email is great, and there's no question that email is always going to work to some extent, but again – email open rates just aren't what they used to be. With chatbots, on the other hand, you're going to get a 90%+ open rate. It's also a great resource to do research and find out your audience's wants and needs directly from that audience. You can ask really specific questions and create personalized funnels based on their responses.

This does take some time and effort to actually develop, but doing so can give you an unparalleled ability to give your customers exactly what they want, to create and sell products that are specific to them. This will, in turn, increase your conversion rates on the back end.

So I think we're going to see more chatbot-based engagement as well as more Messenger ads soon, because the News Feed is getting overcrowded. It doesn't have the same effectiveness as it did, say, three or four years ago: CPMs are increasing, prices are increasing, and knowing this, Facebook is looking for other ways to expand. Chatbots and Messenger are two of those ways; WhatsApp is another.

WhatsApp is a new channel that was recently added to the Facebook Ads platform. WhatsApp is great because it gives you the opportunity to target people based on geographical location (and then directly engage them with Messenger ads). It's going to be huge for both e-comm *and* local businesses.

Going back to Messenger: when you're interacting with your audience in real time, it changes the content of the conversation, as well as the way that audience converts. It's a lot like the little pop-up they have on websites that allows you to start chatting with a live operator, which have always helped with conversion. What this means is that, if you're in the e-comm environment, you really need to incorporate Messenger into your process, even if you find that people don't purchase right away.

If you're running ads and you're creating and segmenting your audiences the way you should be, even just engaging with those people who don't necessarily convert is useful. For example, let's say I've got a video that's a minute long, and a bunch of people watched part of it. I would take that list, and create an audience of people who watched 25% or 50% of that video, then create a strategic remarketing sequence.

This sequence might contain a direct response type of ad sent to those people that engaged with the video, to try to move them from Facebook onto the site, and get them to actually purchase. Then, if they haven't purchased within, say, a 3-day timeframe, I can follow up with Messenger ads that say something like, "I see that you checked this out, but for whatever reason, you haven't completed your purchase. Did you have questions about this product or service that I can answer, to help you come to a decision?"

This allows you to get real-time feedback, data that you can then use to optimize your front-end and overcome whatever challenges are getting in the way of potential sales.

CHATBOT AND MESSENGER "DON'TS"

Chatbot rule #1? Don't spam!

I've seen a lot of people create and launch chatbots without taking the time to actually create custom content. The result is basically a random spam message that says, "Buy here!"

That's a quick way to lose a potential customer. If you're looking to use a chatbot and Messenger to help you increase sales, it's worth taking the time to actually write a sequence that engages your audience in a powerful way, and make it into something that enhances the customer experience.

Don't use them to just try to pitch your offer or make a sale – misusing the tools like this could easily backfire. Instead, figure out what the need is, see what the concern is. Also when you're doing your broadcast, try to personalize things based on how people have responded – basically, create segments within your audience. You can create segmented sequences based on how your audience responds when you do a mass broadcast as well. That way, instead of sending everyone the same message over and over, you're reaching out to only those people who've engaged.

BASIC RULES FOR USING SEGMENTATION

At a minimum, you want to segment people based on a few factors.

The first one is engagement (i.e. the type of ads I'm running). If I'm running, say, a video ad initially, I'm going to create an audience of people that have had 25% or 50% video engagement. I'm also going to create an audience of people who have engaged with or clicked on that ad within the past 7 days.

I'm creating very specific audiences, and time frames around those audiences. I may also create a 15-day and a 30-day time frame based on those segments, and then create sequence messaging that corresponds with each one of those. So, for example, if I see that some people clicked or engaged with that video ad within the first 7 days, I'm going to run a customized message to those people, incentivizing them to come back to the site and take me up on my offer. Those who don't click during that first 7 days' sequence get moved into the 15 days' sequence, and now I need to try to engage them with a different message.

This new message is specifically designed around the fact that they didn't engage during the first time frame. The conversation would consist of a Messenger bot posing a series of questions to try to determine what concerns they had. Then, after engaging with those people, obviously the bot would present them with an offer based on the categories and logic of their responses.

If those people still haven't converted at Day 30, then I'm going to make them a possibly ridiculous offer, but one that's still based on the responses that they've provided.

This process may sound somewhat complex, but it's actually not at all difficult to do. It's really just a matter of setting up your audiences, deciding on the corresponding time frames, and creating the messages for each step.

FACEBOOK ADVERTISING IN 2019

Chatbots and Messenger are going to continue to grow throughout the rest of 2019 and beyond.

Plus, the expansion into WhatsApp chat ads is going to have a huge impact on e-comm. WhatsApp is a huge channel with a separate audience – there are billions of people on WhatsApp who don't use Facebook, so there's no overlap. This opens up a massive opportunity for advertisers, allowing them to tap into a new market of people that they would not have been able to reach otherwise.

Instagram is also going to continue to grow, especially for Millennials and Gen Z users. We're starting to see more brands and a lot more people transitioning from Facebook to Instagram as well.

Online streaming is going to become progressively more important in the coming months. Facebook is gearing up to enter the streaming video arena. Their ultimate objective, of course, is to get people to spend more time on the Facebook platform. So, as users become more comfortable with episodic streaming video, Facebook will no doubt start competing with other (attention-distracting) streaming services like Netflix, Amazon, etc. Obviously, once that happens, more people than ever will be watching videos on Facebook, so this is a really good time to start coming up with an in-stream video strategy.

LEVERAGING AUDIENCE NETWORK ADS

One of the things that I've always hoped Facebook would do is become real competition for Google. I've worked with Google Ads for a long time, and it's still the 800-pound gorilla in the industry. They have so much reach with the Google Display Network, and in some ways, Facebook's Audience Network has been the response to that. However, the challenge with Audience Network is that you only tap into it if your phone is active on the platform.

Personally, I sometimes use Audience Network. I know a lot of people think it has "trash" traffic, but you have to realize that the targeting of people is still the same. The only difference is in the way they're engaging with your ads – you can build up audiences through the Audience Network fairly cheaply, and then leverage retargeting to reengage those people.

So don't discount the Audience Network, especially considering that the News Feed is getting more and more crowded every day, which is going to force people to start using some of those other placements.

Also, the right-hand column. I'm frankly amazed that more people don't use the right-hand column to run some of their ads. For certain types of ads and campaigns – especially for something targeting desktop – the right-hand column absolutely crushes it. Plus, your CPMs are going to be way cheaper than through News Feed, so it's worth keeping in mind. Advertisers sometimes forget about the old-school methods, the ones that have been there from the very beginning, but that's a mistake – many of them still work, and depending on the parameters, can be immensely effective.

To take full advantage of the Audience Network, you need to take a two-pronged approach. The first one involves leveraging Audience Network for cold traffic (because it's much cheaper than the News Feed), then creating a retargeting list from that. So you're basically just using it for engagement, and to provide some on-going brand marketing (i.e. people will keep seeing your brand's ad over and over). Next, you would create a retargeting campaign from that list, and reach them in News Feed and/or a right-hand column ad. This is a good strategy for getting a lot of clicks comparatively cheaply.

The second approach is to reverse the first. So, if you've built a retargeting audience off of, say, video ads or News Feed ads, when you actually create your retargeting campaigns, incorporate the Audience Network into them. You'll get both traffic and sales from that. Just make sure you're looking at your reports – you can evaluate all your sales data, and they'll tell you where your sales are coming from if you have your pixel and custom conversions set up properly.

CUSTOM EVENT CONVERSIONS

I'm a huge believer in custom conversions, especially custom event conversions. People typically use custom conversions with URLs, but I've I found that when I set up custom *event* conversions, my data's always better. That's because custom event conversions fire directly off the pixel; when the data comes from URLs, you're going to have some variances. From a technical standpoint, it's inevitable.

When using this feature, each step of the funnel should have its own very specific custom event conversion, and you should create audiences off of that. This way, you can retarget your people based on where they are in the funnel, and then also create lookalike audiences to scale up.

ADAPTING, MAINTAINING, AND INCREASING PERFORMANCE

In my experience, there are two primary factors that allow a company to survive and thrive. These are simple, but they're also integral to your success, and should be the foundation of pretty much every single digital marketing effort you make.

The first is: test everything. When in doubt, don't be afraid to test. When not in doubt, test anyway.

We can get in the habit of just doing things the way we've always done them, like "if it ain't broke, don't fix it." But in the digital marketing world, you should have a budget for breaking stuff. What I mean by that is, you should be testing a variety of placements and ad types to make sure you're taking advantage of every opportunity, and you should absolutely have budget allocated for that.

The second is: know your numbers. A lot of people run campaigns without actually knowing their numbers.

I'm a big believer in establishing KPIs, especially in the e-commerce world. At any given moment, you need to know your Average Order Value, your 30-day Customer Value, and often, your Lifetime Customer Value. It's very difficult to scale up in e-comm if you don't have those metrics.

So how can you establish those metrics? Don't be solely dependent upon the Facebook pixel, because there are always going to be discrepancies. UTM parameters attached to the links that you're sending people to from your ads are very useful for this purpose.

One of my favorite platforms for tracking (especially in e-comm) is Wicked Reports, because it tracks all the data based on the contact records. It performs the same basic function as Google Analytics, but is much more user-friendly.

Here's why this is so important: let's say I was running the Shopify platform and Facebook ads, and I checked an ad set's performance on Facebook. According to Facebook, this ad set produced $500 in sales. If I stopped here, I would probably think, "Great – let's scale that baby up!" However, if I kept going and looked at the UTM data and the actual contact record of how much revenue was generated, it might turn out that ad set was actually losing money!

A lot of times, people will make decisions off of the first source they see. The information you use to make these decisions will be much better and more precise if you have multiple layers of tracking, and having a tool that provides that data – especially the aforementioned Average Order Value, 30-day Customer Value, and (eventually) Lifetime Customer Value –makes it much easier.

TOP 4 STRATEGIES FOR E-COMMERCE COMPANIES IN 2019

Here are my top four strategies for e-commerce companies to focus on for 2019. I've touched on some of these things a bit earlier, but those things? They're worth repeating!

Strategy 1: Multi-channel marketing is hugely important for e-comm because it's all about adding that personal touch.

For example, if you're selling a higher-ticket item in the e-comm space, getting a phone number should be absolutely critical in your marketing process, especially when it comes to dealing with people who have engaged but haven't purchased yet. So for example, if I'm selling mattresses that start at $500 (or $800, or whatever), I'll give people some sort of bonus or discount or something to incentivize them to give me their contact information. That way, I can incorporate SMS (almost as important as Messenger, as it has the same 90%+ open rate), voicemail, and/or broadcast message follow-up. Or I could have a member of my sales team actually pick up the phone and call these people as well.

Lead ads are another great way of incorporating multi-channel marketing into your overall marketing strategy. A lot of e-comm people don't run lead ads because they think, "Well, I'm not going to pick up the phone to call people," but they really should! This is especially true if they sell higher-priced items. If you're selling something that costs, say, over $200, it's worth a phone call to a potential customer.

Strategy 2: Expand your audience with custom event conversions. Use these to create very specific segments of the audience, and to create lookalike audiences.

Strategy 3: Diversify your approach. Don't just stick with plain link ads; expand into all the other placements too. Just be strategic about how you do it, and keep testing it. Use all the different channels (Messenger, multi-channel video, WhatsApp, etc.) available to you. Use chatbots and leverage video to build and engage audiences.

Strategy 4: Don't be a lazy marketer. Concentrate your efforts on figuring out what your audience wants, and giving it to them. Create sequences so your offers are as customized as possible. Create an experience and an environment that makes customers feel genuinely cared for, and they'll make it worth the effort.

Do you want to see how we have a 1500+ Return on Adspend in a competitive E-Commerce market? You can learn how to get back $15 for every $1 spend on Facebook Ads by going to **www.cvoaccel.com/success.**

CHAPTER 11

Trevor Chapman: The King of Disruptive Digital Marketing

My name is Trevor Chapman, and a year and a half ago, I discovered the life-changing potential of digital marketing done right!

Before I had this epiphany, my focus was on brick-and-mortar sales, with a core competency in disruptive marketing in the "real world." In other words, I specialized in finding and solving a need people didn't know they had, which made it possible to sell the corresponding solution at any perceived value. And I was pretty successful at it – over the course of my brick-and-mortar career, I generated over $100 million in revenue for my companies. But as I quickly realized when I entered the online space, this was nothing compared to the potential revenue that could be made with digital marketing.

My story began in 2005, when I took a summer job as a door-to-door pest control salesman. One thing led to another, and before I knew it, I'd risen through the ranks of the company. By 2008, I had offices at 3 different branches in California, Florida, and Arizona. Everything, in short, was going really well.

Then the 2008 recession hit, and like a lot of people, I lost everything. Tens of thousands of customers, dozens of employees – *gone*, just like that. It was one of the worst experiences of my life.

I took two important lessons away from that crucible: 1) I'm stronger than the self-doubt that I experience when things go very wrong (which, when you're an entrepreneur, is going to happen, and probably more often than you'd like), and 2) that I was in an accessories business, not a necessities business.

Most businesses are accessories businesses, offering goods and services that customers want when life is going well, but which they quickly stop buying when money gets tight. Once I realized this, my mission was clear: I needed to figure out how to switch over to a necessities business.

So I shifted away from pest control and focused my efforts on launching businesses that filled an actual need, not just a desire. Over the next few years, I moved from commercial fire monitoring to defense systems to solar power. One thing led to another again, and by 2016, I owned the largest solar installation company within a five-state area.

One day, the company's marketing department staff came to me to say, "Hey, we need more money."

This surprised me. I said, "You guys have spent your marketing budget, you're supposed to be making money. But so far, you spend money and you lose money. So let's talk about why you need more money."

To their credit, they gave me a reasonable list: they needed more to pay for SDM, PPC, SEO, etc., etc. And it dawned on me – they were engaging in query-based and search-based marketing. In other words, they were waiting for the need to already exist, then competing with other companies to fill it.

With this type of approach, if two customers go to Amazon and type "toothbrush" into the search bar, there's a good chance they'll choose the same thing: the toothbrush with the highest quality at the lowest price. That means the vendors selling that toothbrush are engaging in a race to have the lowest price for the same item, fighting over pennies.

This struck me as pretty ineffective, and a good way to waste marketing dollars. So I decided to experiment with an idea I'd been considering: Is it possible to go screen-to-screen online, like you go door-to-door in the real world?

When you sell door-to-door, you engage in disruptive marketing – you don't wait for them to want it; you bring it right to them. You're then able to imbue the product with any perceived value that you can effectively illustrate. If this is done right, then in that toothbrush scenario, you can convince the customer to choose a $15 toothbrush with a higher perceived value, instead of a $0.99 toothbrush from a random list. In fact, if you do it correctly, not only would he buy the more expensive toothbrush, he would be proud to spend $15 for it, because now that he's an educated consumer, he understands why it's worth every penny, and why it's so much better than the $0.99 option.

So, while just about everyone else I encountered in online sales was focused on selling their products at dirt-cheap prices – engaging in searching online or search-based marketing – I decided to try a screen-to-screen approach where I could reach potential customers directly via their phones through Facebook.

It turns out my experiment worked! Without any prior experience online, this marketing method earned $1 million within 90 days, $2 million 90 days later, and led to an 8-figure buy-out within 12 months. To give you a frame of reference, Facebook itself only raised $2.5 million after its first year in business. This was huge!

When I tell people about how quickly everything clicked into place once I figured out the right marketing strategy, they inevitably say something like, "Man, that's quite the overnight success story!" Which always seems really funny to me – whenever I hear that, my first thought is, "Yeah, I remember a few hours of that long night, that 15-year night that lasted forever!" Because while my success online seems to have snowballed quickly, the reality is that I've been an entrepreneur since 2003, and I owe my recent successes to those early years. I took all the lessons that I learned in the brick-and-mortar world and applied them to my online marketing plan.

This ended up giving me a huge advantage over the competition, as most of the online sellers I encountered didn't have the same real-world experience to draw from. As a result, they approached the business from a very different perspective. Here's a prime example: when I was first starting to shift my attention to the online arena, my buddy, Russell Brunson, told me, "Ugly pages convert better than beautiful pages."

That made absolutely no sense, yet he's someone with more than enough experience to know what he's talking about. So I set out to figure out how something so counter-intuitive could possibly be true. I sent millions of unique visitors to my own sites to try to understand what caused this phenomenon. Eventually, I realized that it's not that ugly pages convert better; it's that beautiful pages take too long to load!

When people click through a site, chances are high that they won't be willing to wait. In fact, in 68% of site visits, the visitor leaves before the page has a chance to load. So how do online marketers combat this? When we see that potential customers have left, we follow them all over the internet, attempting to retarget them with 10% or 20% discount offers. However, these same people, having left the previous site so quickly, often don't even realize what the offer is for – that discount is meaningless to them without context. This scattershot tactic has been the standard response to visitors leaving a site for years, but unfortunately, it isn't particularly effective.

Realizing this, I took a step back and decided to try a different approach. As I mentioned, prior to my transition to the online space, I had spent 10 years recruiting, training, and managing over a thousand door-to-door sales reps.

Part of that training included how to handle initial disinterest. If a customer doesn't respond right away at his front door, you don't just walk around to his back door and repeat the same pitch – it won't change the result.

Instead, you look at customers' behavior, then segment them and figure out what the real issue is. For example:

- Did they visit all the pages except pricing? If so, then pricing wasn't the problem.
- Was pricing the only page they visited? Then clearly, that was their primary interest.

As technology improves, so does your ability to really get to the core of what your customers want. There's so much you can do now! For example, you could separate out the people who spent the most time on your site – say, the top 25% – and segment them based on elements like, "Did they Add to Cart? What did they Add to Cart?" and so on. You can segment it to the point where you know with almost complete certainty what it was that stopped them from completing the purchase. Of course, this sort of deep dive into the metrics takes some time to set up. But if you take that time to really figure your customers out, you'll experience hyper-growth.

However, not everyone sees the point in putting in the extra effort. Over the years, marketers have learned to follow a basic set of all-purpose procedures: whack customers with this banner ad, hit them with that email, smash them with another Messenger message, and eventually you'll wear them down and they'll buy. And because the online sphere has been (relatively) uncongested, this approach has worked. It's also easy, so the thinking is, why do extra work if you don't have to?

As a result, marketers have overlooked a crucial point: that the messenger is just as important as the message. In fact, it might even be *more* important. It's human nature to believe that quality will always win out; however, the reality is that an inferior product with superior marketing will always outperform a superior product with inferior marketing.

WHY SEGMENT NOW?

The online market is maturing and, as with all things, a new era requires new thinking to stay ahead of the curve. As online sales increase exponentially, so do the number of sellers attracted to it. What happens when all of these sellers are equally available to potential customers? It becomes either a race to become the absolute cheapest, or a situation where "the cream rises to the top."

The first option is a non-starter for smaller businesses, because the large behemoths can – and will – bury them. Elon Musk spent $3 billion to earn $1.5 billion; he traded $1 for $0.50. Wayfarer, Amazon, and Chewy are notoriously unprofitable, and yet companies like Wayfarer and Chewy, are being bought for billions of dollars. We live in a world where major players are a) far better funded than you, b) don't care about revenue, only about market share, and c) are willing to go under because they know that eventually, when they sell the company, it'll be someone else's problem.

That's not your or my reality. We as small business owners can't afford to have every dollar we spend only earn $0.50 back – that's a surefire way to go under. So instead, we have to perfect the art of the message, so that when someone else is willing to offer $1 worth of value for $0.50, the customer chooses us anyway, because our messaging is so impactful, they feel like they're getting $100 return on the $1 (or $5 or $25) they spend with us. And that's based 100% on you as the messenger, crafting an eloquent message that resonates with the audience.

HOW TO CREATE A MORE EFFECTIVE MESSAGE

When trying to improve sales, I find that people have a tendency to fixate on the wrong things. We attempt to treat minor symptoms, thinking that will solve the larger issue. We get to the point where we become absolutely convinced that, say, the whole problem is that the "Add to Cart" button is the wrong color or that the funnel has one too many call-to-action buttons, or some other equally unlikely minutia. We focus on these artificial details because, in our minds, the world would be so much better if we could all become millionaires simply by getting all the colors just so, or putting together that one perfect one-time offer (OTO). We really want to embrace that thought. And so we look at our competition and delude ourselves into thinking that the reason they're more successful is that they had 4 OTOs while we only had 3, and that their "Add to Cart" button was pink, and ours wasn't. So if we just fix that, our problems are solved.

The real secret to making your ads more effective is actually really simple – just ask yourself, if you were clicking on your own ad, would you buy it? If the answer is no (as it tends to be about 99 times out of 100), there's your starting point.

The best way for you to get into the right headspace to improve your marketing efforts is to first identify a product or service that you would want to buy for yourself. Then figure out the price point that you would be willing to pay for it if you were in your prime shopping mood. Then, target yourself on the internet. Who were you as a 20 year old? What magazines did you read? What movies did you watch? What pages did you like? What about when you were 30? If you can perfect an ad that would appeal to you, you're likely to attract others with similar interests and profiles.

There is so much hyperbole right now around hustling and grinding and "#beast mode," and I agree with it up to a point. My greatest asset for the first half of my professional career and as an entrepreneur was my willingness to work hard. If someone else worked for 5 hours, I worked for 10.

But it goes beyond that. Working hard and putting in the hours, building the funnels, writing the copy: that's just showing up for practice. It's not the hardest workers who get drafted onto the professional teams; it's the players with the most wins. Now, they might very well be the hardest workers, but it's entirely possible that they're not – hard work alone doesn't necessarily guarantee success.

It's so much easier to think, "If I just work hard and hustle and grind, everything will work out perfectly." You look at someone super-successful like Gary Vee, who posts things like, "Instagram, what's up? This is day 17 in a row that I haven't gone home, I have not slept in 4 weeks, I've got 3 more meetings! Hard work, '#freaking beast mode'!"

Seeing something like this, it's really tempting to tell yourself, "Okay, that's all it takes! I just can't go to bed for, like, 3 weeks straight," but unfortunately, that's just not how business works. The bottom line is, if you want to change what you're doing, you have to *win*. I know that this is a very unpopular sentiment right now – everyone gets a participation trophy, right? But, unpopular or not, this is the reality of the situation.

Facebook doesn't send you a buyer just because you participated; you have to earn that championship ring. And whether online or in the real world, you earn it through a collection of disciplines, the most important of which (for now, at least), is the messaging. If you get the messaging right, you win – it's that simple.

This core concept is firmly rooted in human logic, and has actually existed for as long as commerce has. Throughout history, messaging became increasingly important as markets expanded. For example, let's say you were a fisherman in a village a couple of hundred years ago. If nobody else was selling fish in the marketplace, you didn't have to worry too much about your message. Once you caught the fish and brought them to the public, you really wouldn't have to do anything other than let people know you were there. You could just hold one up and yell, "Hey, I've got fish for sale here. Who wants fish?" Since you're the only one there, you don't have to try too hard – as long as people want fish, you're fine.

Eventually, though, another villager would no doubt try his luck as a fisherman, and would also stand in the marketplace, yelling that he's got fish for sale too. There would be a little competition, but it probably wouldn't change things much from your perspective, as there would still be plenty of customers to go around.

However, markets rarely exist in a vacuum, and if the second fisherman succeeded too, pretty soon a third and fourth fisherman would show up at the marketplace. By that point, it would be quite a bit harder for any of you to sell your fish, as customers suddenly have a lot more choice. Seeing this, the fourth guy, who's newest on the scene and hasn't gotten used to simply yelling that he has fish for sale, might try to draw the customers' attention. He could build a nice little stand, get some entertainment going in the background, etc. – in short, create an environment that gives customers a little something extra as they buy their fish. This would probably entice some of your customers over to his stand, and they'd start buying from him instead.

At first, this might seem unfair to you. After all, you'd been there longer – you shouldn't be losing out just because the new guy has a gimmick! You might then try to get those customers back by insisting, "I've been here the longest, my fish is the best, I go where no one else goes! These newcomers have vastly inferior products! I deserve to win because my fish comes from the deepest part of the ocean!"

Now, this might work to some extent – some customers might be convinced to go back to buying their fish from you. But your situation would still be precarious because your message was about you, your needs, and your claims of superior fishing prowess. You might be right and this claim might be true, but that doesn't necessarily mean your potential customers believe you, or care. In general, as far as the public can tell, you and your competition all sell the same fish, and are therefore interchangeable.

In order to win out over the other fishermen, what you'd really need to do is focus the message on the fish itself. If you could find a way to make your fish sound mouth-wateringly delicious – make it so buyers can practically taste the fish before they even buy it – you would create a lasting impression that would allow you to win out over the others.

DEALING WITH CHANGE

Darwin once said that, "It is not the strongest of the species that survives, nor the most intelligent that survives. It is the one that is most adaptable to change." Change is inevitable, and in order to stay vital and relevant, you must be flexible enough to adapt to it as quickly as possible.

When change happens, the best thing you can do for yourself and your business is to treat it as an opportunity. When the Facebook algorithm changes, don't waste time posting dire predictions about how this will ruin your business and make your life difficult; look at it as a chance to increase your market share or increase your value to customers. This one change in attitude alone will give you a leg up over competitors who are panicking that the new way won't work, wasting precious time with clickbait-type Facebook posts about the horrors of the new system, angrily inviting others to comment and like and share, etc.

The reason that this is a waste of time is that, for the most part, once Facebook has changed something, they're not going back – they have a large-scale plan in place, and they will keep moving towards it. Like many large companies (some of which have business plans that span the next 300+ years), Facebook's goals are far-reaching and intergenerational.

They're not looking for someone to buy them; they're looking to expand their own portfolio by buying companies like Instagram and WhatsApp. So while they do, of course, value revenue, Facebook has bigger, longer-range plans in place, and will make whatever changes they deem necessary in pursuit of those goals.

The other reason that learning to adapt successfully is so important is that the global business landscape is changing at a very rapid pace. I recently met with one of the most successful businessmen in Southeast Asia. This is a man who went from being a fisherman to becoming the second US dollar billionaire in Indonesia. According to him, you and I live in the future. What we in the U.S. consider to be commonplace will reach them in 2 to 3 years.

So what does that mean for us? Here's an example: Facebook buys Instagram for $1 billion. Instagram's a Tier One app, meaning that most of its users are in Tier 1 countries, and it's growing at a rate that can outpace Facebook. What does Facebook do after that? They buy another app, WhatsApp.

WhatsApp has almost no Tier 1 users. Its user base is primarily located in Southeast Asia, Africa, and Eastern Europe – it's an app that's focused almost exclusively on developing emerging markets. Facebook bought WhatsApp for $17 billion, 17 times what they paid for Instagram. They were willing to do so because, going back to our earlier analogy, emerging markets are a place where no one's selling fish yet. There are more connected devices in Indonesia alone than in all of North America combined. Yes, North America's GDP may be larger, but emerging markets' potential is massive, and largely untapped.

Note that, when I talk about the opportunity in emerging markets, I'm not talking about just worldwide targeting ("I'm going to buy a bracelet on AliExpress and ship it to Uganda"). I'm talking about bringing actual value, a quality message, and a quality product to those areas. That's a massive opportunity, and Facebook clearly plans to plant its flag squarely in the middle of it.

So while the market expands every day, and while Facebook makes whatever changes they see fit in pursuit of their goals, it's more important than ever for the marketer to learn to adapt quickly. The internet is a massive echo chamber with lots of parrots everywhere, repeating what people are saying. It's filled with consumers, but very few creators. Every day, there are more and more people offering fish for sale. In order to thrive in this new reality, rather than spend your day yelling, "Buy my fish! Buy my fish," you need to be publishing content into that echo chamber yourself.

Most of it, no one's going to hear – a lot of content simply won't resonate. But if you publish regularly (preferably multiple times per day), eventually something you post will stick. The internet has this wonderful quality where, if your message is timely and relevant to even a fraction of your audience, they will engage. And once they engage, they'll share it, and it will spread exponentially. In 2017, the average active social media user had 140 active social media user friends. If you posted something that resonated with even one of them who shared it with friends who then also shared it, by the fourth generation, you would have reached 2.7 million people.

This is a very powerful tool for the small business owner. You can't compete with companies that have massive budgets allocated for awareness campaigns that have no return on investment, who can casually spend tens of millions of dollars on Superbowl ads and the like.

But what you *can* do is post as much content as possible. Whether it's a sentence, a photo, a video, or a long-form post, keep disseminating content until you find what resonates. When it resonates, dig deep with that message and mine that vein until it runs dry. By doing so, you create a tribe, and with that tribe, it's easy – once you've built that group, you can easily figure out how to serve them, what they want, and quickly become their favorite fisherman!

CREATING BETTER MESSAGING

I have a podcast called "The Trevor Chapman Show." When I first started, though, I initially called it "From 7 to 8 Figures" because, in my experience, while you can accidentally make a million dollars in a year, you can't accidentally stumble into 8 figures – that requires deliberate engineering. The goal of my podcast is to share everything I've learned that allows someone to reach the 8-figure mark.

Initially, I did the podcast myself; then, upon the advice of Kevin Rose (the creator of digg, among other sites), started inviting guests to participate, many of whom have mastered the art of the message. While our individual experiences were different, the core tenet was the same – it all boils down to confidence. If you walk into the marketplace with the true conviction that your product is the one your audience needs, and genuinely convince people that it is, eventually they will take your word for it.

My oldest son is 11, and he's reaching that awkward stage where he spends a lot of time thinking, "Oh jeez, what do I do? I want to be cool, so do I stand like this? Or like this?" My wife and I are trying to teach him that nobody knows him better than he knows himself, so his honest opinion of himself will set the tone. If he walks around like he's cool, people will think he's cool, because he obviously knows something they don't. But that works the other way too – if he walks around feeling timid, they'll sense that, and again assume that he must be exactly what he thinks he is. To a large extent, you create your own reality – whatever you believe is going to happen, is likely to happen.

In the same vein, your focus dictates what your life will be. If you watch Game of Thrones every night, you deserve to be a Game of Thrones trivia champion, and you probably are. If you say, "I want to have the ultimate message and be the ultimate messenger," and focus your time and effort on that, you will be deserving of that opportunity. You want to win on Facebook? Deserve winning on Facebook. It's not about hacks or shortcuts – you simply have to show up, roll up your sleeves, and do it. I know that, if I'm only willing to make a sub-par effort, I don't deserve to win – if I did, it would just be an unsustainable, momentary fluke.

MESSAGING MISTAKES COMPANIES MAKE

This is a bit of a balancing act. On the one hand, you want to create something stable and compelling that appeals to customers; on the other, you don't want to get so mired in details that you miss your window of opportunity. So you don't want to cut corners, but you also don't want to sweat the small stuff.

As an example of the latter, a couple of weeks ago, after visiting one of my sites that I'd sold, a friend of mine asked, "Dude, how did this thing even generate revenue? Your 'Shop Now' button is pixelated." I explained that the button had actually been pixelated since Day 1. It never bothered me, because before I do anything, I evaluate each action in term of return on investment.

If I focus on that pixelated button, is it going to bring me a greater return than if I focus on x, y, or z? If not, then I prioritize x, y, and z instead. The pixelated button doesn't matter. If people want an item, the pixelated "Shop Now" button isn't going to stop them from clicking on it. If they don't want it, it's not going to be because of the pixelated button.

In my opinion, too many people wait to launch because they want every tiny aspect to be perfect, and often focus on the stuff that doesn't matter.

Ultimately, your best bet is just to get the message out, and let the market tell you what it does and doesn't like. It doesn't matter where a random comma goes. What matters is whether or not the market says "yes" and buys it. In the end, that's the only thing that matters, and you'll never know that unless you put it out there.

Then, once your message is out there, iterate, iterate, iterate! This needs to be done continuously. One of the mistakes I often see people make is, once their message is disseminated and marketers start to see a little bit of success, they sit back and rest on their laurels, assuming that they've hit upon the magic formula and the success they've experienced will be self-sustaining.

So they stop paying attention, then all of a sudden something gets shut down on Facebook, or an algorithm they use gets changed, or Pinterest pops up, etc. Suddenly, they've lost their audience, and they're completely unprepared.

In this industry, you simply don't have the luxury of thinking, "Well, I've paid my dues, and now I get to rest. I've created the message, and should now be able to sit back while it generates income on its own." Unfortunately, that's just not how it works. Those dues were paid yesterday. Today is the only thing that matters, and today has had no dues paid.

WHAT SMALL COMPANIES SHOULD STOP DOING

At this point, I firmly believe that companies should steer clear of hit-and-quit, one-and-done transactions. They should be focused on creating lifetime value in everything they do, and on fostering the tribe.

Again, the bottom line is accessory versus necessity. An accessory is a non-essential, and often something that's bought once and probably never again.

Now, if you happen to be a large company – if you're Wayfair or Chewy – that's fine. But small businesses need to be selling consumable products. And by that, I don't necessarily mean food products – I mean that we need to be engaging in something that doesn't require us to have to find new customers every day in order to avoid unemployment.

We need to be finding products and services that allow us to go back to our same customer base, and convince them to buy again and again. We need to focus on the long-term, not just what's popular right now. For a while, fidget spinners were a hot "it" product. But if you choose that as your product, what happens when they lose their appeal? As soon as fidget spinners are "out," you're unemployed again.

We're much better off focusing on building our businesses like the large tech companies, with an eye towards longevity. When choosing a path, we should consider things like: How can I make this last for 100 years? If I'm going to pass this down to my kids, what's it going to look like?

You want to grow a forest, not chop down a tree. If you build your company based on that concept, you'll end up with something that will take care of you, and it's far more likely to sell in the long run (if you choose to go that route), because businesses with long-term potential are attractive prospects.

THE "DOS" AND "DON'TS" OF FACEBOOK MESSENGER AND CHATBOTS

Messenger and chatbots belong to a new channel on Facebook and, like all new channels, offer an amazing opportunity for a company to get massive traction. In addition to being new, Messenger is *relevant*, and needs to be focused on right now in order to take advantage of what it has to offer before it becomes oversaturated.

When using these, I would concentrate on transferring the customer information into something that I own. Facebook owns the applications themselves (as well as any data collected through them), and can decide to change or eliminate the apps at any time. If you only focus on building your bot subscriptions without getting a copy of the data that you can control, you run the risk of having all your hard work be for nothing. So find a way to get your subscribers to opt-in, and then give them enough value so they'll reply with their email addresses and other relevant customer data. If you do this religiously, you'll have a lasting result from this new medium.

At the moment, people are using Messenger to broadcast massive messages all the time. It's pretty much a given that Facebook will regulate that soon – it would be naïve to think otherwise. But for the moment, you can take full advantage of the platform, get as much of that information into your own hands as possible, and when the changes inevitably happen, you'll be able to rest easy knowing that you maximized the opportunity.

It's also extremely important to use this platform with as much innovation as possible. To return briefly to the fish analogy – remember that people stopped listening to the fishermen who used the same tactics as everyone else. The multiple cries of "Fish for sale," day in, day out quickly become a kind of white noise to potential customers. By the same token, if you blast everybody every day with an offer and they're not interested, people will start unsubscribing. Facebook is designed to notice the volume of unsubscribes, and you're going to lose access to this marketing channel because of this flawed approach. So be very deliberate with your approach on this new placement, and maximize your return – it's not going to be available forever, so use it very intentionally while it lasts.

THE FUTURE OF FACEBOOK

Undoubtedly, Facebook and other platforms like it are the future. They already shape our perceptions and cultural touchstones to an unprecedented extent, especially in the youngest generation. My kids, for example, have no clue who Oprah is, but they're well-acquainted with YouTube fixtures like Logan Paul.

The question is, how do we understand the changing times and capitalize on them? Eventually, we'll get all our information through our devices, and be able to control what content does and doesn't reach us. That's the normal course of events for humans in general – we advance with an eye towards being able to avoid the things we don't like. Originally, if we wanted to travel across the country, we walked or rode horses. Then we built trains to speed up the process, then cars to allow ourselves more freedom, and now we fly. We took something that used to be a grueling, months-long trek with a 50/50 chance of survival, and cut it down to approximately 6 hours of mild annoyance.

Our progress is due in large part to our built-in desire to avoid anything that wastes time or energy. The same is true online – as technology becomes more sophisticated, so do consumers. If you are a marketer who only focuses on sales, sales, sales, sales, sales, eventually you'll become the equivalent of a fly-over state. If you don't put some effort into creating and maintaining a bond with consumers, they'll simply learn to avoid you.

I have a buddy who has a site that gets a million organic clicks a day, all off of his Facebook fan pages (of which he probably has 100). Now, he didn't create the fan pages because he loves Game of Thrones and the other TV shows they feature. The fan pages are purely a means to an end, a way of getting clicks, which is how he monetizes his site. But the people in those fan pages have no clue that this is the end goal. They don't know that this obscure website has anything to do with the fan page. Instead, they see this value, something that speaks to them.

This is the magic of the internet – its ability to give you unprecedented access to your audience. You have the opportunity to compete for people's attention in vast numbers right now, the kind of opportunity that you could only have gotten by buying a Super Bowl ad not too long ago. This is a golden era – the internet is mature enough that you don't need to write your own platforms, but still young enough to be the Wild West or the Klondike.

There are still areas where you can plant your flag and claim your territory, like in the early days of the gold rush. And if you do it right, people will want to visit your territory and consume your message. They get value from your content, and you get a loyal, engaged audience in return – everybody wins.

The key, though, is to make sure you're always offering consumers something valuable. To extend that metaphor, there are a lot of areas that I can see are going to turn into ghost towns. They're cool right now, but they don't have long-term value.

I'm going to use Logan Paul as an example. Logan Paul is a famous YouTube vlogger who's all over TV and the internet right now. The bulk of his audience consists of 8-year-old boys. This is how young the internet is – Land Rover paid him $150,000 for product placement on one of his vlogs, despite the fact that his audience is mostly made up of 8- and 9-year-old boys.

Why would a company like Land Rover choose him for product placement, even though his audience isn't anywhere near old enough to drive, let alone buy an expensive car? Because Logan Paul has a proven track record of getting attention. He then takes that favorable attention and uses it to push people to a store to buy his merchandise.

Recently, he was involved in a controversy that caused his YouTube channel to be temporarily demonetized. He immediately stopped vlogging as often, and the number of views and new subscribers on his channel has since declined.

The takeaway here is, as you build your own railroad tracks to your planted flag, make sure you're always looking at the process from the consumer's perspective. After all, if it's not a destination people want to visit repeatedly, no one's going to ride that train.

THREE E-COMMERCE STRATEGIES TO IMPLEMENT RIGHT NOW

As I mentioned, throughout most of my working life, I was basically just an offline marketer. It wasn't until I started to associate with people with much more experience under their belts that I truly began to understand what a successful business strategy looks like. Seeing how these companies operated, I realized that my one-and-done mentality wasn't doing me any favors – it was bringing in money now, but doing so at the expense of tomorrow. Once I understood this, I took great pains to change how I operated, and how I applied the tools of my trade.

The three most important strategies I implemented were as follows:

#1: Facebook should be an acquisition platform – its primary function should be acquiring new customers.

You should then gather as much of that data as possible, and use it to build the rest of your foundation outside of Facebook. Utilize it here and there to retarget, etc., but first and foremost, Facebook should be used for what it does best – gaining new people. Once you acquire them, you can follow them to other, cheaper channels where they spend their time, and turn them into a community, into repeat buyers, etc.

We are so focused on finding the hot new product – it's the fidget spinner mentality again. It works up to a point – those who sold fidget spinners in their heyday probably made a lot of money and maybe bought themselves some expensive toys. But now, that product is no longer viable, and these same sellers are frantically looking for the next fidget spinner.

During that same period of time, other sellers focused on a sustainable business model. Maybe they found some amazing shampoo or organically-sourced coffee. They might not have earned as much money in the short term, but they're not scrambling to figure out their next step now either. They focused on acquiring customers, and then implementing a longer-term strategy.

They didn't stop with acquisition, with a one-time sale. Instead, they spent their time, cultivating those customers, indoctrinating them, communicating with them, finding out what they want – basically building a successful feedback loop between themselves and their customers.

#2: Engage with your customers in ways that others don't. Find new and innovative ways to connect with them. Go out there, start (metaphorical) fires, film everything, and put the videos on your Facebook page. Then drive the visitors from your Facebook page back to your website, and create a forum community where people return repeatedly, not because they were in a one-time buying mood, but because they think, "I love this. This is content I really want." Build your own network, basically. This is so important. If you don't like doing this, hire someone else to do it – just get that content out there!

#3: This is loosely related to strategy number two. Whether you're doing personal or company branding, you need a constant, steady stream of new content. Here's an easy way to do this: visit your competitors' sites, and see what they're writing and making videos about. Make a list of the 100 most recent titles. If you can't find enough of those, go to BuzzSumo or some other research and monitoring tool, and look up the top titles that people clicked on over some period of time. Write down 100 of them.

Then, take 3 days out of every 3-month period to focus exclusively on making off-the-cuff content. You can film yourself with your phone, have someone else film you, go to a studio – whatever makes you most comfortable. Spend those 3 days filming 3- to 5-minute clips of you talking about each topic. Take a title like, "This is Why You're Broke," and just spend a few minutes ranting about it. It doesn't have to be perfect, just interesting.

Now comes the tactical part! Organize the videos, then go to Rev.com (or the transcription service of your choice), and get all of them transcribed. Have the transcriptions embedded into the videos. Put the full version of each video on YouTube, and a shorter version of each – with 720 x 720 dimensions and bars above and below – on Facebook. I found that I get incredible engagement this way, far more than when the text isn't included.

Then take the text from each video, and break it into shorter pieces. Take a paragraph or two and use it to create a short version of the content, typed out in a short-form or long-form social post. Use the full transcription to create a blog post. Finally, pull 3 sentences from each video and create 3 different quote cards with them. These can encompass anything – "This is Why You're Broke," or, "This is Why You Won't Survive a Zombie Apocalypse," or, "This is Why You Need Creatine," etc. Again, don't worry too much about the topics; just make sure that each is one is attention-grabbing.

So off of one 3-minute video, you now have:

- Two videos (a shortened one for Facebook, and a long one for YouTube),
- A complete transcribed blog post,
- A long-form post for Instagram and Facebook, and
- 3 quote cards

Do this for every video, then mix-and-match and upload. On Monday, put up the YouTube cut of the first video, the long-form text from another video on Instagram, and the quote card from a third video, etc.

Just make sure that you don't upload two versions of the same video in a single day. As long as you have a month or so between, say, a video and its corresponding blog post, no one will realize that it's the same content because they're consuming it through a different channel.

Break the posts up throughout the day. At 8am, post a quote card; at 12pm, a video; at 4pm, another quote card; at 7pm, a third quote card; at 10pm, the long-form post. Do this daily, making sure to separate content from a single video.

By making those videos over the course of 3 days, you now have a full business quarter's worth of content. They won't all be gems, of course. But you'll find that one or two pieces of content from that quarter will resonate deeply, netting you hundreds of thousands of followers and thousands – maybe even tens of thousands – of shares. And the more you do this, the better you'll get.

Then, you can always boost the posts to increase their reach. The trick is to do it strategically.

In my business, while I might spend five bucks on boosting posts here and there, the bulk of the budget is reserved for posts that strike a strong chord with my target audience organically. If I post a video, for example, and it gets a minimum of 2,500 shares for every million views, I know I have a winner on my hands.

This is my basic ratio for page post engagement decisions, which can be scaled for each individual video's view count. In other words, going by that ratio, if you have a video with 10,000 views that got at least 25 shares, it's worth spending money to get it to go viral. If it's below that ratio, the video isn't engaging enough to garner sufficient organic interest for you to get a 4 (or 5, or 6, or 20) times ROAS, and therefore not worth spending the money to boost. If, on the other hand, you have a video with, say, a million views that gets 10 thousand shares, that's your cue to forget the budget and throw everything you have behind it – that post is going to end up being a goldmine.

I'm focusing on videos here, by the way, because I believe that they're the most universally appealing medium for getting your message across. They offer the widest variety of ways to consume content – if you prefer to read, they have subtitles; if you like to listen, there's audio; and if you want to watch, well, they're videos!

STRATEGIES FOR ACQUIRING LEADS WITH FACEBOOK

A friend of mine in California had his first $10 million day last year, using only Facebook ads. He sells gold, silver, and other precious metals, and for years, he was operating in the low 7 figures, until he decided that it was time to take it to the next level. One day, he just said to himself, "I'm going to make it happen."

So he took his entire budget and focused it on acquiring customers on Facebook, and then used other means to close those leads, to target them offline through direct mail, etc. Shortly thereafter, thanks to Facebook, he made $10 million in a single day. He will break a billion dollars in the next 8 months solely due to Facebook Ads.

So if you're worried about whether or not you're going to pay rent this month because people aren't buying your fidget spinner, open your mind to the idea that it's because everyone else is selling a fidget spinner too.

Take yourself out of the fidget spinner business, and instead ask yourself, where is there a need? Where is it being underserved? Be that first fisherman.

Go out there, sell the fish, get better at it, and dominate the market. Figure out where your customers are, and find a way to get their attention.

If, for example, your target audience is outdoorsy, figure out where they spend their time, and target them there. But don't overlook the less-obvious choices: your male outdoor enthusiasts might not be on Pinterest, but their wives probably are. So while you're reaching out to the men, you can also put together something like a "Top 10 Gifts to Give Your Lumberjack (or 'Bear Grylls Wannabe') Husband." Use email, Messenger, text messaging, and any other direct means you can think of to reach your customers.

Wherever people's attention is, that's where you need to be. You need to find a way to put yourself between the thing they're focusing on and them, and redirect their attention to you.

THE SHELF LIFE OF INTERNET MARKETING STRATEGY

Part of the process of creating a long-term, sustainable plan for yourself and your business is building in a degree of flexibility. There are two major components to any business plan: strategy and tactics. Change comes to this arena at lightning speed, and you need to be ready to reconfigure your tactics at a moment's notice. But if you've found the right necessity-based product or category, and commit to keeping your message and content fresh and engaging, your strategy should be able to last you for the foreseeable future.

Tactics change constantly. The next Instagram could come out tomorrow, and blow up, like it did before. It wasn't that long ago that everyone was super focused on Snapchat, and now practically no one uses it anymore.

So the tactics will change, the how-to will change, but the principles will stay the same. Our early ancestors ran around trying to hit each other with rocks, but those guys inevitably lost when they eventually came up against guys with bows and arrows. And the ones with bows and arrows were, in their time, wiped out when guys with guns came along. While the underlying motivators are always the same, the methodology changes, and you have to be able to evolve if you want to survive.

The good news is that you're a master adapter! Humans are at the pinnacle of the animal kingdom due to our incredible adaptability. We're aware of the fact that we're self-aware – when you think about it, it's kind of mind-blowing. In practical terms, this means that not only can we change based on our own experience, we can learn from the experience of others and incorporate those lessons into our plans. And through this amazing ability, we can learn to let go of the fear of the unknown, and respond with agility to any unexpected changes that come our way.

SUMMARY

So, to sum up the lessons I learned over the last 15 years that have helped me successfully navigate the field of internet marketing:

- As Glengarry Glen Ross famously taught us, "ABC: Always Be Closing."
- Find an unmet need and fill it – don't waste your time with accessory businesses.
- Set yourself apart, and cultivate flexibility.
- Contribution-based marketing will always win the day.
- The law of reciprocity is phenomenal with customers, associates, and mentors. So always be contributing. If the focus of your message is to add to the well-being of your customer and your audience, you will eventually succeed.

Do you want to see how we have a 1500+ Return on Adspend in a competitive E-Commerce market? You can learn how to get back $15 for every $1 spend on Facebook Ads by going to www.cvoaccel.com/success.

CHAPTER 12

Rory Stern: The Compliance Artist

My name is Rory Stern, and I've been a full-time digital marketer for the past 11 years.

Over the course of those 11 years, I became proficient at Facebook advertising, learning everything I could about copy, funnels, optimization, and the underlying psychology of the consumer.

This business wasn't part of my original plans. After finishing graduate school and getting a doctorate, I was gearing up to go into a profession. I quickly realized, however, that if I did that, I'd never get to see my family. Whatever else happened, I wasn't willing to sacrifice that time with them, so instead, I decided to become a stay-at-home dad.

I fell into digital marketing because it offered me the opportunity to provide for my family on my own terms. I needed to be able to reach people, to provide value, to make an impact, and to do something in this world, while still being able to help raise my kids and make money.

Even so, it wasn't an easy choice. Digital marketing is a cutthroat industry. The sheer volume of information that you need to be able to process at any given time is daunting. While I was getting my bearings, my family was my touchstone – if it hadn't been for them (well, and my own sheer stubbornness), I probably would have given up and gotten a job. Instead, knowing that this was an opportunity that would allow me to be present for my kids, I stuck with it and took my lumps, believing that it would all work out in the end. It took some time, but once I got a handle on the business, I never looked back.

I tell you all of this because I've been seeing a really disturbing trend lately, where "experts" basically tell people, "Yeah become a Facebook advertiser. It's easy!" I'm here to tell you: No, it's *really* not!

Conversions, keeping up to date with the latest tools and platforms, navigating the constant changes... you know, I've spent 11+ years in the trenches, and I still don't even think of myself as an expert. I consider myself just an advertiser, trying to stay on the cutting edge as much as the next person, doing my best to sustainably build and scale real companies. Doing so requires constant study and diligence. It may be rewarding, but there's nothing easy about it.

If you want to be successful in this business, one of the most important traits you'll need to cultivate is the ability to remove the emotion from what you're doing. I really struggled with that in my first business, because I was so emotionally tied to it. That takes a real toll on you when things don't go the way they're supposed to, as they often don't. In order to be able to stay with it, you have to get to a point where you're not emotional about the results.

Once you're objective, rather than blaming yourself or getting disheartened when something goes wrong, you'll be able to look at a situation and think, "Alright, this didn't work. What can I learn from it? How can I improve?"

The reality is that very few strategies work perfectly right out of the gate; most need testing and tweaking in order to be effective. It's much more productive to be able to treat a negative result as an opportunity to learn from the marketplace, adjust your approach, then try again. Business is not emotional, and there's nothing to be gained from beating yourself up over a less-than-optimal outcome.

FACEBOOK ADVERTISING TRENDS

The most obvious recent Facebook advertising trend is the dramatically increased competition. And with more people jumping on the advertising bandwagon every day, costs are rising all the time, and will likely continue to do so because that's just the way advertising works in the digital space.

The good news is that, well, to be blunt, most people suck at advertising. So two things are going to happen amidst this more crowded platform:

1. If you're smart, you pay attention, you don't succumb to bad advertising practices, and don't get caught up in the hysteria over rising costs, you'll find ways to beat the people who suck at advertising, and

2. Facebook is going to slap down all of the scammy, scummy marketers who suddenly materialized out of thin air as Facebook became an increasingly popular advertising medium. I've been expecting this backlash from them for months, and I figure it'll happen any day now.

One of my mentors was a very well-known media buyer. People were constantly asking him, "Where's the line? And how close can I get to it, how far can I push before I get in trouble?"

His response was always the same: "Forget that! Know where the line is, stay the hell away from it and ask, 'How can I create better ads and more compelling offers without having to go anywhere near the line?'"

I firmly believe that, just as Google brought the hammer down on advertisers years ago, we're going to see big changes happen with Facebook ads. And it's going to be a great opportunity because the cream is going to rise to the top, while everybody else is going to be left in the dust.

HOW TO BECOME THE "CREAM"

One thing that's become very clear is that, even in this day and age where an unprecedented number of marketers and advertisers are running Facebook ads, people don't know policy. It sounds obvious, but surprisingly few people have thought to learn it. So start by reading Facebook's policy guide.

I make a point of reading it at least once a month. I have a copy printed out and sitting on my desk at all times. And you have to be diligent about keeping current whenever a new version comes out. It's not Facebook's job to make sure you follow up when one of their rules has changed; it's your job to stay compliant.

It's also really important to understand the fundamentals of what it means to be on Facebook. Most regular people (i.e. non-marketers) go to Facebook to get away from their problems, to get away from reality, to share cat pictures, to look at kids, maybe to rant and rave about something going on in the news. They're not there to be sold to.

If you're a marketer who understands this basic principle, you understand why running plain ads where the message is pretty much, "Buy, buy, buy, buy!" wouldn't be ideal. That's not what this platform is about. A lot of people miss the mark – this kind of tone-deaf advertising happens more often than you might expect.

Can you make money off of Facebook running those ads? Yes. Can you build a company off of them? Sure.

But one of these days (and that day probably isn't too far off), Facebook is going to crack down, and you're going to get slapped or shut down, and you're not going to know what to do.

However, when you target the right way and present a product the right way, you can strike gold. I can't tell you how many products I've bought off of Facebook that I didn't even know existed, that I was never looking for, but when they were brought to my attention, I had to have them! And it's never been the hard-hitting, edgy, hype-y copy that convinced me to buy; it's always been something that subtly makes its way into my head or tweaks a passion that makes me think, "Wow! That's really cool! I want it!"

MISTAKES TO AVOID

As far as I'm concerned, the Number 1 biggest mistake people make on Facebook is not familiarizing themselves with the policies.

Take, for example, ads for weight loss products. Facebook clearly states that you can't talk about weight loss and dieting. They also specifically prohibit "before-and-after" pictures. Yet advertisers keep talking about losing weight and using before-and-after pictures in their ads. So either these people haven't read the policy guide, or they got caught up in the idea that other people are getting away with it, so why shouldn't they be able to?

Another example: it's against the rules to run ads in Facebook groups. That policy is kind of hidden – it's not explicitly spelled out – but running ads in groups is not compliant. When I mentioned this recently, someone replied, "Well, I see ads in my groups all the time!"

And while I'm sure that's true, that doesn't make it right.

Of course, the same person also commented, "But then again, I'm getting ads for cannabis, right now and I know that's not compliant."

So, basically, familiarize yourself with the ad policies, and stop worrying about what other people are doing.

Another mistake to avoid: don't crowdsource Facebook for advertising advice. You've got to find a mentor, a system, a training module; something you can follow. Because I can guarantee you there are, like, 15 different people out there teaching 25 different systems.

They all work, but only if you pick one of them and stick with it. They're all built on a foundation, or a theory, or a result. You can't pick and choose bits and pieces here and there unless you *really* know what you're doing. Don't just funnel hack, don't just swipe and deploy; know *why* you're doing it. Keep an eye on the bigger picture. As far as I'm concerned, this is a fundamental rule.

There's a Facebook buyer's group that I visit pretty regularly, and one of the most frequent questions that comes up is, "What's the best course to take in order to learn how to do this?" There are always a few people who reply with something like, "Oh, go through the Facebook ad blueprint, it's free."

And yes, absolutely, if you go through the Facebook ad blueprint, there's probably some solid information in there. But if you have a specific goal in mind, this might not be enough – the information lacks context. They give you the basics – which, again, are always helpful – but the blueprint isn't necessarily tailored to a specific goal you may have. If you want to learn direct response marketing or brand advertising, you probably won't be able to get enough information that applies to your specific circumstances to form a working strategy just from this.

Free training is great – I went through plenty of free trainings when I was starting out. But at some point, you may want to start investing in people who are getting results, because they can provide you with a more detailed, goal-specific roadmap. So, again, don't crowdsource your planning – you're much better off finding a single source who's found something that works well, and model that system. Just make sure you have a backup plan (or 6) ready to go too, just in case.

Something else to avoid: relying on a single traffic source. That's just common sense – the all-eggs-in-one-basket approach is dangerous. I mean, there *are* people out there who make a good living off of just Facebook, and they might continue to be able to do so. But there is so much traffic out there that's better than Facebook ads that people just aren't tapping into.

That said, Facebook has a lot going for it, and it's easy to see why it's so appealing to advertisers. For starters, the people are there. There are tons of people who are on Facebook constantly.

Then, of course, there's the targeting that Facebook allows you to do to get to know the users' likes and dislikes, to really let you tap into social conversations. This is immensely important – the social interaction component has shifted online in such a huge way over the last 10 years, it's truly amazing.

And though there's obviously a pretty steep learning curve, the Facebook platform has an ease of use that's unmatched by any of its rivals. I'm talking specifically about things like targeting, the ability to turn ads on once you know what you're doing, and the ability to get results within 24 hours. As in, you can actually tell within 24 hours whether you're on the right path or not. I often tell people, "You give me $100 and 24 hours and I'll let you know whether we've got proof of concept." The way Facebook is set up, you can see what the market's telling you at lightning speed.

There are, for all points and purposes, two schools of thought when it comes to e-commerce. The first one is all about trying to make huge profits as quickly as possible – "Oh, you can you can make a killing practically overnight! You can make six figures! You can make millions!" It's the new Wild Wild West of internet marketing, a land of quick-turnaround push-button riches.

Then there's the other school of thought, which doesn't get a lot of attention because it's not as sexy. This one says that, when you go out and spend that money, it's about the long-term. It's not about the short-term payoff; it's not about running, for example, t-shirt ads with the mindset of, "Let's run as many t-shirts as we can. Even if their designs are a trademark infringement, let's make money. When we get shut down, we'll start again."

It's easy to see how this might be tempting – that t-shirt scenario works. I'm against it because I don't believe in trademark infringement and the get-rich-quick approach, but the business model can work for some people.

Personally, I think it's far better, more rewarding, and generally less nerve-wracking to build something with a stable foundation that can stand the test of time (and where everything you do is legal).

Going back to the $100 and 24 hours idea – you want to focus on not wasting money when you're improving your metrics, when you're identifying breaking points in your funnels.

For example, we ran ads for one of our clients. In the first month, we spent $7,000, and got $0 back. On the surface, that would seem to be a dramatic failure. We approached it as a learning opportunity instead. We took what we learned from that data: "Okay, we can get people to move to our website, we can get people to 'Add to Cart,' but we couldn't get people to buy." What does that tell us? Was the traffic the problem, or was the data telling us that there was something fundamentally wrong with the checkout process?

So we went back, we put our heads together, and based on our findings, recommended a course of action to the client. And the next month, we turned on traffic, and the same $7,000 expenditure turned into $30,000.

The point? You're never wasting your money if you're learning something, if you're taking away valuable information. And it doesn't have to be at the $7,000 level. You can apply the same philosophy with $100. Just make sure that you're taking all the factors into consideration. For example, if you're selling a $5,000 product and you spend $100 on marketing without getting any results, well, I mean, come on, with a product that expensive, it's going to cost more than that to get a sale.

It's all relative, and the takeaway here is to establish a (reasonable) proof of concept, pay attention to what the market tells you as you zero in, bring it back in-house, and say, "All right, what do I do next?"

WHAT COMPANIES SHOULD DO TO ADAPT TO FACEBOOK'S NEW DEVELOPMENTS

A lot of training programs tell you to just go straight for the sale. And if you can get that going, that's awesome. I certainly built a company off of going straight for the sale, where we have one funnel. But the funnel that ends up working for you isn't always your first funnel, right? It could be your 15th funnel. So what happens while you're working on funnel 2, funnel 3, funnel 12? You need to have more going on.

As far as I'm concerned, the gold mine is always lead generation. You need to be generating leads of people that are interested in your product constantly. Just because they don't buy again right away, doesn't mean they won't buy again.

I like to do lead generation followed up, of course, with email marketing (smart email marketing). We have to make sure we're treating our customers right. And again, we can do all this with ads.

How are you following up with your customers? Are you sending them coupons? Are you offering them discounts? Are you upselling? Are you cross-selling? You need to be more proactive in engaging with your audience than just, "Buy my t-shirt! Buy my t-shirt! Buy my t-shirt!" Because when you do the latter, you're basically just putting up a billboard and hoping it pays off.

Again, I'm not knocking this approach – I've seen it work time and time again. But in my experience, it's just not sustainable. You need a solid client acquisition funnel, and the only real way to obtain that is through lead generation for prospects and buyers.

I happen to love a free-plus-shipping approach. I know plenty of marketers – many of whom I'm a big fan of – who hate them. Which just goes to show that there are tons of different approaches, and any number of ways to build businesses. For your purposes, my way may not always be the right way or the best way, and it's *definitely* not the only way. As long as you focus on lead generation for prospecting and the customer acquisition funnel, you can then absolutely go straight to direct-to-sale, and have it work beautifully.

Controlling the path to conversion via acquisition funnels is key – you can't simply rely on your store or site to do the work for you. When we decided to build a business that had a Shopify store, we actually didn't start with a Shopify store. We started with $0 in the bank and 0 customer lists, and since we were direct response and info marketers, we opted to play to our strengths and start from list building. We built a customer list, found out what they wanted, and only *then* built the Shopify store in order to fulfill those wants. This is a really simple principle, but one that applies to every single business to some extent. It's also how I suggest starting any business: build your list, find out what the people on it want, and go out and give it to them.

We did this with Facebook Ads, tried a bunch of different things, and started selling them products. It took a while, but we finally found one funnel where, when we put in $1, we got $1.75 or $2 back. We built a nice 6-figure-a-month business off of it, but that was the tip of the iceberg – the real money is in the back end. So after we zeroed in on the right funnel, we followed up with the Shopify store and emails.

I think one of the most brilliant strategies I ever heard when I was a struggling marketer and really didn't get it came from an interview with Mike Hill, a marketing strategist, a few years ago. During the interview, Mike told a story about a guy who sold guitars on eBay, and was having a really hard time of it. After struggling for a while, this guy thought to himself, "Well, what is it that guitar users need? How do I identify guitar users?" The obvious answer? Guitar picks. So he started selling guitar picks on eBay for $0. He knew that anyone buying guitar picks was a guitar player. So after the sale, he would follow up with the pick buyers via email and in his eBay store, telling them, "Hey, I also sell guitars."

You really need to start thinking outside the box; outside the traditional approaches that everybody else is taking. When I tell that guitar pick story, a lot of people who hear it are very concerned about the idea of giving something away for free, about losing money on a transaction without getting anything back. But that's the point – you do get something back: the customer's attention. The goal of this type of strategy isn't to give something away for free; the goal is to get to break-even.

We did a free plus shipping promotion with an item that cost us $7.95. If you factored in our advertising and shipping costs per unit, we ended up losing money if someone bought just that front end product. However, we also included 3 upsells. That changed the picture considerably – out of all the people who got the free item, we only needed a small percentage to also go for the upsell in order to offset the cost of the entire promotion. So if you walk away at break-even, you're in the homestretch because now you've got a back-end and you can sell them more products.

So be willing to take a loss on product number one, as long as you've got upsells.

And again, you definitely want to focus on prospect acquisition and customer acquisition with the funnels.

WHAT COMPANIES SHOULDN'T DO, EVER

First and foremost, again, you should never ignore ad policies. Don't run non-compliant stuff.

Next, don't sell bad products. Just don't. Low-quality merchandise, cheap knockoffs, stuff that basically exists to take advantage of customers – these are a terrible idea from start to finish. You want your business to be perceived as an ethical company, one that customers can establish a relationship with. That will never happen if you piss your customers off by selling them crap.

Another big "don't": don't ignore customer feedback. I see it all the time: store owners and/or their team members either don't read or don't pay attention to the comments about their ads. This is a social world you're advertising to, and if you're not interacting with your customers and you don't know what's going on, you're sunk.

Typically, the first couple of comments that show up are positive; they boost conversions. If they're negative, however, that tanks conversions. If you're not paying attention to comments, you're missing out on what's happening in your business. When there are comments like, "The coupon didn't work" or "This product is terrible" or "I've contacted customer support but they're not getting back to me," these are all problems you can get out in front of. So make sure to read the comments, respond to the comments, and most importantly, learn from the comments.

If someone claims they wrote to you but haven't heard back, a quick response of, "Hey, I'm sorry we didn't get that email. Can you please private message that page?" or "Send me your phone number and I'll call you right away" can do wonders. That's an opportunity to turn a complaint into a compliment. And most of the time, the people who complained will post a follow-up message along the lines of, "Wow they actually called me and took care of my problem." Just like that, you've restored your credibility, and people reading the comments are going to think, "Okay, it's safe to do business with them."

FACEBOOK MESSENGER AND CHATBOTS

Although I love the potential of Messenger bots, I don't incorporate them as much as I probably should. When clients first started asking about them maybe six months ago, I still thought of them as non-essential – a fad that hadn't had all the bugs worked out yet. The jury was still out on whether they would end up becoming more than that. We were doing really well with the existing tools, so there was no rush to introduce this new element.

However, over the past months, the bots have improved markedly. Every day, more and more of our clients request bots to be added to their strategy, and we've started to take them more seriously as a means of engaging with the audience. They should absolutely be something that you're looking into, and figuring out how you can use them to their best advantage.

The most basic bots are already built into Shopify, where you offer shipping updates through Messenger. Shopify also lets you browse catalogs and order right in Messenger. Those built-in functions create a more streamlined buying process for customers, and that's huge.

The more advanced bots – ManyChat, Chatmatic, Chatfuel, etc. – are where the excitement is. They let you build out sequences you use in your ads to get people to comment, automate basic administrative functions in Messenger, and have any number of other applications. I haven't explored them enough to have a grasp on the full scope of their potential within the industry. We've mostly used them to create posts like, "Comment, 'Made in America' if you want to receive a coupon for X % off." This helps build social proof and engagement. You can certainly use those posts to create engagement audiences to retarget to people. That's something I would look at doing at a bare minimum.

Having this tool available to create social proof is great. Hopefully, you make sales. You do want to be careful when using bots like this, though, because you're adding an extra step to engagement. It's an extra move; it's an extra click. So you can end up getting very cheap comments of, "Yes, I want the coupon," but then are people actually going to use it?

You want to weigh the pros and cons of this process before you implement it. Again, we go back to one of the fundamentals: Don't just use it because it's there. Don't just use it because everybody's raving about it. Use it because you have a strategy, and a way to measure the results of that strategy.

In general, I've always thought that just "winging it" was a bad idea. The only way an approach is going to work is if you put some put some time, thought, energy, and effort into it. It also helps to look at how successful people are doing it.

I have a client right now who wanted to incorporate a Messenger bot. He was very eager to move forward with it as quickly as possible. My response was, "It's not a bad idea, and you seem really enthusiastic about it, which is great. Do you have a specific goal or objective in mind?" He didn't, as it turned out – for the most part, he'd just heard that they were the next big "thing," and he wanted to be part of it.

This isn't a comment on bots' usefulness overall. There are plenty of people and companies – even clients of ours – who have entire auto-responder "choose your own adventure"-type systems using bots. They're really sophisticated and they're really smart, but again, the question we always have to ask ourselves is, do they lead your customer or your prospect down a path to a good experience and/or a measurable, trackable ROI?

Obviously knowing your target audience – their demographics and psychographics – makes a difference when deciding whether to incorporate this tool into your process. It basically all boils down to, are the people you're targeting tech-friendly? Are they Messenger- friendly?

During a campaign where we were running ads for an older demographic, I was really interested to see if they would engage. As it turned out they did, they really did! The comments, the social proof from this age demographic, were through the roof. But when we looked at how many of them opted in, how many clicked, it was dead. In that case, a traditional drive to a squeeze page or a pre-sale page, was the clear winner. So again: always look at objective, measurable results.

You can also ease into the transition by creating a kind of hybrid approach. You could mix some more traditional components into the Messenger bot technology in order to improve the customer experience. For example, you could send a customer an unboxing video review to make them feel better about what they just purchased, and they'll remember the experience (and your company) because of it.

A lot of people in our space are drop shippers. I'll tell you right now, even though I've done it when I had to, I absolutely hate drop shipping. Customers don't want to wait 3 weeks for a product; they want it *now*. But, if they *do* have to wait, how can you reduce anxiety and potential buyer's remorse in the meantime? Something like an unboxing video could go a long way.

FACEBOOK ADVERTISING IN 2019

Obviously, costs are going to continue to go up.

Then, I think we're gearing up for a big backlash. We've seen the beginnings of it already in the announcement from Mark Zuckerberg. That announcement didn't actually mention advertising at all. Everything he talked about concerned organic reach.

But at the same time, while the new rules don't apply to ads directly, they indicate sweeping changes across all of Facebook, and the altered dynamic is going to affect ads too. The response was staggering. There was mass panic. Facebook's stock plummeted.

Facebook is a living ecosystem, and although, again, the changes officially only affected organic reach, the algorithm did change. And I watched as countless peers and multiple accounts of our own – all previously high performers – unexpectedly dropped. Suddenly, CPAs were going through the roof, campaigns were drying up, and people just didn't know what to think.

When a metaphorical wave hits your ad account, the best course of action is to remove emotion, finish the work, and do a post-mortem afterwards. What happened? Did your CPM skyrocket? Did your relevance scores drop? All of those things matter. And when you're able to remove yourself from the equation, you can get a grasp on the situation. In this case, those of us who did so realized, "Oh, it's the timing of this announcement, something with the algorithm changed."

In general, when things of this nature go wrong, there's no way to know what single factor caused the problem; we just have to accept that it happened, and now it's time to get to work and start fixing it.

TOP 3 STRATEGIES FOR E-COMMERCE OWNERS IN 2019

Honestly, it's all about the fundamentals, the basics. Prospect list generation, customer acquisition, direct-to-sale to encourage lifetime value – for Facebook ads, that's what it's all about. All the tactics I've talked about, they're all just means to achieve those 3 goals.

In terms of prospect generation, I love giving out a first-time customer coupon. I also love running contests, where you take your core product and give it away for free. And again, this comes down to proof of concept. You find a product that your customer would pay for. Ideally, this is an item with a high perceived value for your customer, something the customer would want to actually go out and buy from a store, and preferably, something that would cost a lot in the store, but which you're able to acquire inexpensively.

For example, we ran a contest featuring an item that would cost $50 or $60 in stores, but we were able to pick it up for $15. That was a great choice to use as a prize – the thought of winning a $60 widget just for entering your name and email address or Facebook ID is very appealing to people.

The idea here is that you're building a list of prospects, you're finding out what they want, and then you're selling to that list. We ended up building a list of 35,000 people, and we sold a lot of that $60 widget to them off the back of that contest.

There's a company called UpViral that specializes in this sort of promotion. We tested UpViral with our contest. Our contest was the 'ad to landing page (or "squeeze page") to thank you' type, which said, "Thanks so much! We're really excited to be announcing the winner on such-and-such date. If you just can't wait that long, you can order one for yourself today at 25% off the normal price." We got to break-even very quickly just by having that self-liquidating offer there.

When we saw how well that worked, we thought to ourselves, "Imagine how much better this would have gone if we got UpViral adding in other people to spread the contest." So we got UpViral, and our list did grow, but the quality of our leads just absolutely plummeted. That's not meant to knock UpViral – they're great at what they do; it just didn't work for this specific promotion. This is why you've got to test everything – it's the only way to know for sure.

Although it didn't work out in that particular case, I love, love, love contests – it's an excellent resource for list building. It's all about that strategy, that funnel flow, how you get your people going through your world.

Coupons are another great way to build lists. Offer people 15% or 20% off a first order, then track whether people are actually using it. Do you need to have follow-up in place to make sure they use it? That's always a great incentive, and people love it.

Any of these are potentially great for building prospect lists. Customer acquisition, free plus shipping, really deep discounts (50% to 60% off) – anything that gets them into a funnel is great, then upsell, upsell, upsell. As long as you know your strategy, your numbers, and what you're willing to spend, it'll work.

Then, once you have these customers, you need to make sure to really take care of them. Customer support is majorly undervalued, when it really should be a top priority.

You can't be robotic with your customers. You can't just send them to a FAQ. They want to hear from people. A lot of times people just want to know that they're heard. E-commerce is growing like wildfire right now, and there are so many marketers jumping into the arena – the overall effect makes consumers hesitant, suspicious. It's why so many people love Amazon. They know and trust Amazon; they don't know the rest of us yet, and can't trust us right away.

We had a client who set up his page so that, if you messaged it with a question, it would spit out a FAQ response. And if you called their phone number, they were met with a message that basically said, "Go check out our Facebook page." The minute we had a team member take over management of his social media and customer support functions, his refunds went down from 15% to 5%. In other words, just take care of your customers, respond to them, treat them like human beings, and they will love you.

This is also why it's so important to read the comments on your ads. People will tell you exactly what they want. Take that stuff seriously. It's crucial to follow up with customers – after a customer buys something, send an e-mail asking them, "Did you like it? Any problems?"

Like many people, I buy from Amazon because I'm busy, I'm on the go – I have a business, my wife works, I've got kids – we don't have a lot of spare time. And I just don't like going to a brick-and-mortar store. Shopping on Amazon is just easy – they have everything, they're established, they have free shipping, and my order arrives in two days. It's just a turnkey system at this point; it's reliable.

But I'm also a big t-shirt nut, and there are a couple of companies I buy from because their t-shirts are unique. That's their competitive edge – they give me something I can't get anywhere else.

It's the same with customer service. If you're providing support, 'thank-you' notes, customer-only specials, and generally giving the customers something special, they're going to buy from you because you treat them right. They're not just buying the product; they're buying the experience.

People love experiences. So make a point of going beyond just the transaction and give your customers something to remember. Call your top 10% of customers – get on the phone, call them up, and thank them (or have someone from your team do it). Send a handwritten 'thank-you' note with a chocolate or something. Make your customer feel genuinely, truly appreciated, and you've just forged a meaningful relationship that these people will remember for a long time to come.

Do you want to see how we have a 1500+ Return on Adspend in a competitive E-Commerce market? You can learn how to get back $15 for every $1 spend on Facebook Ads by going to **www.cvoaccel.com/success.**

CHAPTER 13

Josh Marsden: Ordinary Guy with Extraordinary Vision

I'm Josh Marsden, and I'm a normal guy. I was a military brat for the first 11 years of my life, my family constantly moving around the world with my full-time soldier father. Then, when I was 11, we moved to Arizona, and my dad decided to continue his military career in the Arizona Army National Guard. I've lived in Arizona ever since, and at this point – 25 years later – I definitely qualify for full "Arizonian" status.

My parents were hard-working people who believed in the power of education. They believed in working hard, getting your college degree, finding a good career, and advancing in your field of choice. They didn't know much about business, but they taught me about work ethic, discipline, striving for excellence, and character.

I took those lessons from my parents seriously, and followed the typical route from high school to college. However, like many other young adults, I made my fair share of mistakes early on – not taking college seriously, partying too much, etc. – and I ended up stumbling pretty hard.

When I was 19, I dropped out of college after a year and a half, with zero credits. It's pretty upsetting when I look back at it now, but at the time, I was more interested in devoting my time to my first serious relationship and fun with my friends than to worrying about the future. I used to play a computer game called Starcraft all night, until 6:00 the next morning, then go to a 7:40

class with literally no sleep. Unsurprisingly, I slept through quite a few of my classes back then.

Obviously, I was making very poor decisions at this point in my life. Ironically, when I did apply myself, I did really well on my homework, quizzes, and tests. I had all this potential, but as we all know, potential without action is, unfortunately, meaningless.

After dropping out and working odd jobs to make some money, I didn't know what to do with myself. Thanks to my dad, I grew up around military life, so I decided to go back to what I knew and join the Arizona Army National Guard, following in my dad's footsteps.

This turned out to be the best thing I could have done at the time. The military centered me and brought me back myself. For years, I had been drifting away from who I truly am at my core: a goal-centered, hard-working person, with a deep drive for success and excellence. Being in that familiar military environment allowed me to get back on track, propelling me to excel in the air traffic control division, and eventually earning an FAA certification in Air Traffic Control.

Shortly after finishing my certification, I re-enrolled in college. Thanks to my previous stint in college, I was able to earn my first 30 credits by testing out of a bunch of subjects. Then, I threw myself into the courses I needed to finish my degree. I got my bachelor's in about three years, and a few years after that, I even went back and earned my MBA.

After college, I went to work for the University of Phoenix. I had a very successful sales management career there from 2005 to 2012. I pushed myself hard, and was a consistent top performer during my tenure. I had a great group of friends that I worked with, a stable salary, and a bunch of awards that I earned during my time there. But…

The University of Phoenix started changing sometime around 2010, gradually becoming a very different place over the next 2 years. Unfortunately, some of those changes led to a decrease in opportunities for advancement. At the time, I was driven by new challenges, opportunities, and money. When the changes at the University began affecting my career potential, I started looking elsewhere.

I was persuaded that switching careers would be my best bet, so I left academia and joined a software company called Infusionsoft. It took a big leap of faith to leave a secure, nearly six-figure position at the University of Phoenix and plunge into the unknown, but I knew in my heart that I couldn't stay. So I took a deep breath and went for it.

My job at Infusionsoft was in sales. I helped small businesses learn about how Infusionsoft could help them grow their companies. This was my first real exposure to e-commerce; I spent a lot of my time listening to stories about how businesses were making money online, what they were selling, and what niches they were in.

By the end of 2012, I realized I wasn't happy at Infusionsoft. I was back in sales, grinding it out, spending my days unchallenged and bored. I was used to sales management, so going back to sales definitely had an impact on me that I didn't foresee when I made the career switch. I was still doing my job and achieving my sales quota throughout the year, but I was just going through the motions.

At the end of 2012, I was let go, and honestly, I deserved it. The only thing I was doing right was achieving my sales quota; in every other respect, I was a reluctant bystander. I wasn't fitting in and trying to be a team player. I was missing meetings, coming in late, and expressing views that were counter-culture to the team that I was on. I didn't want to be there, and it showed.

I've always been a big believer in the idea that everything happens for a reason, even if it maybe doesn't feel like it at the time. At the end of the day, being fired from Infusionsoft was the best thing that could have happened to me, and led to where I am today. Additionally, regardless of how it ended, working for Infusionsoft was a valuable experience for me – it opened my eyes to new possibilities and career opportunities I never knew existed because I didn't really grow up with any type of entrepreneur influence around me.

Within two weeks of leaving Infusionsoft, I received two job offers (one on the same day that I left Infusionsoft!). Neither job started for some time, so during the gap, I decided to test the waters as an entrepreneur.

I'd had my first experience with entrepreneurship while in elementary school, when I got the idea to borrow classic Nintendo games from kids and lease them out to other kids. So I did have a little bit of entrepreneurial spirit, but I didn't have any type of guidance when it came to building a business and making money on my own, and so had never really revisited the idea after childhood effort. However, I'd been thinking about it a lot during my time talking to e-commerce business owners at Infusionsoft, and given that the jobs I'd been offered weren't starting for a while, it felt kind of like the universe was shouting at me to give entrepreneurship a try – I had nothing to lose!

So I registered as a freelancer on sites like Odesk and Elance (which have since combined to become Upwork), and this became my first foray into earning money without being dependent on a company. I only made about $1,700 during the weeks that I was out of work, but it was enough for me to see that I could create my own opportunities.

After dabbling in entrepreneurship as a freelancer, I started working full-time for a company in a position that promised to pay me more than I'd ever earned before. However, not long after I'd started working, that same promising company gave me an ultimatum – if I wanted to continue working there, I would have to change my parenting schedule. They weren't happy that I left at 5:00 p.m. two or three days per week to pick up my son from pre-school. So I had to make a decision: Do I stay at this company? Or do I bite the bullet and start my own?

Thus followed a series of "pros and cons" lists that would help me arrive at a decision based on sound logic. Of course, in hindsight, I realize that was unnecessary – the decision was a no-brainer, and in my heart, I already knew what I was going to do. There was no way that I could be okay with missing time with my son for a job. But, even though the choice was obvious, human nature dictated that I had to work through all my fears first in order to come to that patently obvious decision.

So, after brain-dumping the pluses and minuses onto a sheet of paper, I realized that I really didn't have so much to fear by committing to starting up my own company. That was my turning point – I quit my job, and went "all in" on starting and growing my own company so that I could support my family while still being the kind of father that I wanted to be (i.e. a present one).

Since this pivotal choice, my company has grown by 40% – 80% every year. Still, just like any entrepreneur, I've experienced the highest of highs and the lowest of lows. I've struggled. I've experienced more stress than I've ever had in my life. But, no matter what happened, I never gave up, and worked my way through any challenge that came my way. It helps that I've got a great team, great entrepreneurial friends, and mentors that have all been there to help me advance my vision. Thanks to their help and my stubborn determination to see it through, we've become a successful, thriving Facebook Advertising and Sales Funnel Agency that helps other small businesses make their dreams a reality too.

In the end, I feel like the luckiest person alive, and am incredibly grateful to be able to be working with one of my passions – digital marketing – while truly making an impact to the clients that we serve.

DIRECT RESPONSE MARKETING

The types of companies I work with are determined by their specific verticals. E-commerce is a big one that my team and I focus on, and we provide value and impact. We also help coaches, consultants, and traditional professional services, like financial advisors, sell their services. Lastly, we help entrepreneurs sell digital products, either through launches or through online funnels and Facebook Advertising.

Regardless of the vertical, direct response marketing and a lot of the facets and disciplines of digital marketing are generally used together. However, in our experience with e-commerce companies, there's a big gap – companies that offer physical products differ from companies that offer digital products or services. They might know about a sales funnel, especially because some of the influencers out there today teach what a funnel is. Some of them may even understand sales funnels from a technical perspective. But for the most part, the majority of e-commerce companies simply don't know a lot about online marketing, and they struggle.

These companies don't understand web design, especially how to create high-converting websites. They don't understand direct-response copywriting. They don't know how to leverage follow-up, and they often don't know how to leverage advertising as effectively as they could.

Although other niches and verticals have some struggles as well, in my experience, it's definitely most prevalent in the e-commerce and professional services niches. Those two niches struggle the most with achieving results from online marketing, which seems somewhat counterintuitive (at least from the e-commerce perspective) because in e-commerce, you're selling a physical, tangible product, and people love buying real products.

From a marketing standpoint, digital products sales require more work, more convincing, and more skill. With physical products, it's easier to see success with online marketing. You dial in on your message, convey that you know your benefits, and articulate those key points in a way that communicates with your target audience. As long as you're communicating about a physical product in a way that gets your target audience to care and want to know more, online marketing success if much easier to achieve, especially if you know what you're doing.

UNIQUE DIRECT RESPONSE MARKETING

What makes my company's approach different from those of other people who offer Facebook or funnel training (or from software that allows a person to do both relatively easily) is that we're skilled direct-response marketers. Direct response is a very high-level method of applying marketing to generate results. There are definitely more companies today that help e-commerce and other verticals implement sales funnels, build out sales funnels, and implement Facebook Ads. However, the abilities and the skills needed to produce results take a lot of work; it takes a lot more study, more effort, more experience, and more practice.

The biggest differentiator between us and some other companies out there that also help businesses build funnels is conversion. Anybody with the right tools (like ClickFunnel or Leadpages) can build a funnel these days. Actually getting a funnel to convert and do well – that's something my company is skilled at. That's what separates us from the rest.

SUCCESSFUL COMPANIES STILL HAVE ROOM TO GROW

I love working with e-commerce businesses that are successful, established companies in their own right, but still struggle with online marketing. They have opportunities they're leaving on the table, and they know it – they're aware that they're not doing as well as they could be doing with Facebook Advertising and using sales funnels to automate their business and marketing.

This is my favorite type of company to work with – large-scale, mega-successful e-commerce companies that still experience some struggles with their online marketing efforts, and who are leaving opportunities behind. For me, it's like stepping into a Ferrari and being the one who can get it to drive at 200 miles per hour.

This type of company needs someone to essentially "own" the online marketing aspect and really help them with Facebook Advertising, sales funnel processes, and incorporating multiple automated marketing funnels through email and chatbots. These things can really complement all their other sales funnel processes, and when it gets going, it's like pouring gasoline on a low fire. The sense of accomplishment is unparalleled – it's why these are my favorite.

CASE STUDY: TEXAS LONE STAR TAMALES

One example of this is our work with Texas Lone Star Tamales. They're a Fort Worth-based company that's been around for quite some time. They started implementing internet marketing years ago, and became a seven-plus-figure company long before they came to us.

But, while they're a successful business with a recognized brand that has solid sales, they were leaving a lot of money on the table, because they weren't advertising effectively. They didn't have funnels or understand direct response marketing. They tried, but they weren't successful, because it's not something you can learn overnight. It takes time to gain that skill. When they came to us, we were able to provide them with a shortcut.

We worked with them through our new client strategy process. It's called our "Double Your Sales Diagnosis." During this process, I consult and collaborate with the business to really identify their opportunities to leverage. We come out of the Diagnosis with one goal to focus on.

This client's goal was to take their big, warm audience and their good-sized email list, and convert leads into sales. We decided to start by seizing the "low-hanging fruit" using an activation funnel.

An activation funnel essentially targets your warm audience, people who haven't purchased yet or haven't purchased in some time. This is the basis of the "80/20" in your market -- the 20% of your market that produces 80% of your profits. You don't want to ignore those people, or to leave them alone for too long. At the same time, you want to be careful to avoid overwhelming the other 80% of your audience – the cold audience (i.e. new people) – by bombarding them with offers before they're ready to engage. They need to be approached differently (and separately) from the warm audience – those new people might become customers, and you don't want to get in the way of that. In short, you really want to focus on a specific segment of your market.

My company went through the Diagnosis with this Texas Lone Star Tamales, and built an effective funnel using our copywriting, design, and marketing automation skills. We also implemented effective email campaigns that only went out in response to behaviors exhibited in the funnel process.

We ran ads into this funnel, essentially building a five-day cash-machine funnel. Our initial campaign saw a 400%+ ROI. Given how successful the first round was, we then repeated the process all over again, and the results were just as successful the second time. This is my favorite type of success story – they were pretty much the perfect e-commerce client, and I definitely have fond memories!

2019 TRENDS IN FACEBOOK ADS

While Facebook Ads and the ability to attract the right people into your funnels will continue to be part of marketing automation and funnel strategy, 2019 is geared up to introduce some new trends.

This isn't the same environment that e-commerce companies were in five years ago. Back then, you could have a great ad and run it automatically long-term – what we call "evergreen" – and it would bring in cold traffic that knew nothing about your company. You could basically invest a dollar and make several dollars back.

Online marketing is no longer like this. We're at a point where you have to monitor your ad performance constantly, and take your brand very seriously in order to have success in most markets.

There are, of course, some less sophisticated, lower-competition markets, that don't require as much effort. With these, you can still get inexpensive traffic on Facebook comparatively easily, so you can still have success even if you don't get everything right.

Ideally, though, even in these markets, you should focus on your brand and have a strong brand. Then, you can leverage all the stages in your Facebook advertising funnel.

I'm a big fan of how Dennis Yu of BlitzMetrics explains it. He talks about focusing on three stages in your Facebook advertising funnel: the awareness stage, the conversion stage, and the monetization stage.

When most people think of Facebook advertising (*especially* in e-commerce), they just think about the conversion stage; they don't think about the awareness stage, and they definitely don't think about the monetization stage.

The awareness stage is about creating and disseminating really good, valuable content that communicates your brand, communicates your message, differentiates your brand, and builds a relationship and trust with people who are interested in what you're offering. In order to do this well, you have to have the right target audience. You also have to have the right messaging, so it's relevant to both the target audience and to the product that you're selling.

Having a good awareness stage and a good brand message is a huge trend right now. From a tactical and technical perspective, you can get really good results by implementing this, because a lot of people advertising on Facebook aren't spending much money on awareness-type content – it doesn't drive directly to an ROI; its primary purpose is to build your warm audience.

That's why you have to have a full Facebook advertising funnel. You need to have ads going out to a cold audience, with retargeting happening at specific stages of your funnel. When they're aware of your brand, when they come to your website, when they've consumed your content, when they've clicked on Add to Cart, when they've clicked in Initiate Checkout, after they've become a customer, how you're following up with them and maximizing the ROI from your customers: these are all stages in a Facebook advertising funnel.

If you're doing all those things effectively at every step, your overall Facebook ad account will be extremely profitable. Which means that you can weather having an ad campaign that isn't producing more than breakeven when it comes to return on ad spend, because you've got other ad campaigns making up for it. This current trend – having a full, step-by-step Facebook advertising funnel process that includes that awareness and the branding, has great conversion ads, leverages retargeting, and also leverages the customer base to maximize ROI – is something that e-commerce companies need to take very seriously.

Another couple of trends I've noticed are 1) that Instagram is being used more avidly; that's definitely climbing right now, and 2) chatbots are also coming to the forefront. They're newer tools, but if you're using chatbots effectively, you could definitely generate some significant ROI from that.

The biggest trend, though – and the one that's going to make the biggest impact on your performance – is the implementation of a step-by-step, layered Facebook advertising strategy. You can't think of Facebook advertising as just one campaign, or just one campaign and one retargeting campaign. You have to think of it as an entire system you're setting up, with several stacks of Facebook ad campaigns.

WHAT E-COMMERCE COMPANIES SHOULD BE DOING TO ADAPT

The most important thing that companies need to do is to plan out their strategy with a layered approach in mind. Before they jump into doing Facebook advertising, they should have a solid plan that follows the methodology I mentioned above.

First, this allows them to be as effective as possible when following current advertising trends.

Second, the technical implementation needs to be arranged this way as well, because it can be very complex when you're leveraging different retargeting audiences and you're excluding audiences. The messaging has to be slightly different at each step, has to be adapted to fit that specific step in your Facebook advertising funnel.

So e-commerce companies must be careful to implement these the right way – by using retargeting stacks and exclusions of audiences, and by writing and creating ads that make sense at every stage of their Facebook advertising funnels.

If they do all of those things, then they'll be able to implement Facebook advertising effectively, and see a solid ROI from their efforts.

WHAT E-COMMERCE COMPANIES SHOULD *NOT* BE DOING IN 2019

First and foremost, e-commerce companies should stop focusing exclusively on conversion ads; instead, they should think of their Facebook advertising as a full-fledged funnel (as described earlier).

I've also found that a lot of e-commerce companies don't have the right mindset when it comes to marketing and advertising. For example, I see a lot of hope-based marketing in e-commerce, where companies spend money on an ad and basically keep their fingers crossed that it will generate a result. They're not tracking it, they're not really concerned with strategy, and they're not writing good, effective copy. Then, when they don't get the results they wanted, they decide, "Facebook advertising doesn't work for us."

This is counterproductive. Instead of running ads off of hope, it would be much more useful to plan ad campaigns strategically in advance, and when they go up, to track and measure the results at every step in the process. Companies should also avoid running singular-mindset-driven ads, opting for a comprehensive strategy instead.

If e-commerce companies stop doing those things, then they're definitely going to fix a lot of the issues that keep Facebook Ads from yielding the kind of results they're looking for.

I also see a lot of e-commerce companies using their websites alone for new customer acquisition. The problem with that is e-commerce sites have *maybe* a 3% average for new customer conversion success rate (i.e. people landing on the website and converting over). If you have an actual acquisition funnel that complements your website (where you're driving traffic to this funnel, so you're controlling the conversion path in a way that you simply can't with an e-commerce site), you're going to see a much better conversion rate. You're also going to see a higher average order value when you're using upsells and downsells and a proper value ladder effectively in an acquisition funnel.

THE FUTURE OF FACEBOOK ADVERTISING

Facebook advertising is getting progressively smarter. A few years ago, you had to set up your ad campaigns in a very measured fashion, where you were controlling the results, rather than letting Facebook's algorithm dictate the outcome.

Now, however, the algorithm has improved to the point where you can publish an ad campaign to a fairly broad audience, say 2-4 million people (or even more) while targeting a single interest (instead of a bunch of interests), and still produce a result. Because the algorithm has gotten smarter about finding the exact right people to show your ad to once it picks up traction (if it's a good ad that generates results, customers, and sales).

The only potential downside is that, because the Facebook ad algorithm's gotten so much better at generating results for companies that are advertising on their platform, there are a lot more advertisers jumping into publishing ad campaigns. As a result, the competition has increased, and will continue to increase even more as the algorithm continues to improve (which it obviously will).

Which means, of course, that the competition for resources and placements is fiercer when you start advertising on Facebook. This will eventually separate the marketers from the non-marketers. In other words, if you want to continue to get results from Facebook advertising, you really need to focus on the ad creative, the messaging, the videos, the images you're using, and choosing the optimal ad types for your business (Facebook gives you lots of options: canvas, slideshow, collection ads, dynamic product ads, etc.). You need to leverage all those factors in order to produce the best result. In short, you have to become a better marketer to adapt to the future trends that are already starting to happen.

On top of that, you really need to focus on Instagram as well. Study it, get to know it, get familiar with it from an advertising standpoint (not just from an organic one). As of now, it's still a (relative) bargain, with cheap acquisition costs for acquiring leads and customers, especially on Instagram Stories. To date, there's not a lot of competition on Instagram Stories, so it's a fantastic platform for e-commerce companies to advertise on.

The comparative cheapness and relative lack of competition aren't going to last, so now is the best time to jump into Instagram and get to know it. You'll want to be a seasoned Instagram advertiser by the time it gets crowded, so you already know what works on there and are then able to "outmaneuver" your future competition.

TIPS FOR MAINTAINING/INCREASING PERFORMANCE

Here's a good tactic, especially for a low ad spend budget: if you're an e-commerce company that doesn't have a monstrous ad spend budget, drive traffic – even a cold audience – directly to your offer. If they don't convert, retarget them with brand-type content. You're building a relationship with the people that showed interest in your brand, your company, and your product from your initial ad. So, retarget them by communicating your brand differentiator, your process differentiator, your product differentiation, and also telling them about you.

This way, you're what Scott Oldford calls "omnipresent" – you're creating an association with these audience members as the owner of your brand, because when they've already shown some interest in your product, all those combined factors are going to drive them to buy. And you can also set it up so that you're retargeting them after they've consumed your brand content with an ad based on the offer they last saw. At this point, you can also sweeten the deal a bit – you can maybe add a bonus or give them a discount, and then drive them back to the offer. That's a strategy that works really well on the front end of Facebook advertising.

Another tip: use dynamic product ads. A dynamic product ad is a smart ad that shows customers new products that are related to products that they've purchased. So, if someone bought Product A from your website and now you're retargeting them because they're a customer, a dynamic product ad will show that customer Products B and C, which are related to and/or complementary to product A.

So, let's say you have five different product images in a dynamic product ad showing. If you have your pixel set up comprehensively – not just set up in the header, but actually set up throughout your entire e-commerce site and your funnels – Facebook's going to learn what people have purchased from you before. Then it will show products to the customers you're targeting in the current ad campaign, choosing which ad to show to whom based on those previous purchases.

Just showing your customers dynamic product ads works really well – it's typically an instant ROI-producing campaign. It's fairly easy to implement, to write, and to produce the creative content, and it can generate a significant ROI.

Another strategy that's particularly good for product validation – so this is good for brand new e-commerce companies that are trying to get some traction for their product – is to set up a contest with a landing page. You can set this up yourself, or use Upviral, an application that makes the setup quick and easy.

The contest should promote, for example, a free giveaway of your product. To enter, prospects go to the landing page and enter their email address. The prize can be your product itself, or the product with bonuses, or some sort of bundle – whatever you think will work best. People love free stuff, especially if you have a great product and you're matching that product with the audience that you're targeting. Ideally, your audience is already interested in your product, especially if you build interest in it in your ad as you are promoting the call to action to enter the contest. Keep the contest open for, say, two to four weeks – no more than a month.

In the end, one lucky winner walks away with a free product, and you walk away with a bunch of emails belonging to people who are already interested in your product! Now, you can follow up with them, and offer them an incredible deal to purchase the product they were interested in winning. It's a winning strategy that works really well for validating a new product.

You could also use this contest as an activation funnel strategy. You can use that same process for people who have come into your funnel and have purchased in the past, but not in, say, the past four-plus months. Or for people who never purchased, and have been in your database for the past four-plus months. Segment those people, and then target them with that specific funnel and that specific marketing strategy – it can pick up a lot of traction in that scenario as well.

WILL THESE TIPS AND STRATEGIES CONTINUE TO WORK FOR THE FORESEEABLE FUTURE?

While there are no guarantees, of course, I can't imagine a scenario where these don't work anymore. The first strategy I went over – using dynamic product ads – is in line with the trends happening on Facebook today, as well as the direction that Facebook seems to be heading in. That said, Facebook innovates continuously, and ad creative, content, and messaging options continue to evolve.

But while the names of the tools that Facebook releases and the formats of the various ad types may change, the underlying purpose of them – to introduce people to a company's products and brand message in a way those people are comfortable with – will always remain the same. Those are the elements that are going to raise e-commerce companies to the top of the Facebook "food chain," provided they can quickly adapt their strategies according to any shifts in the overall Facebook ad protocol.

As for the contest idea, I don't see any obstacles there. After all, it's basically a lottery, and the lottery's been around for how long now? Times may change, but human nature doesn't. People will always love to win free stuff, and are happy to enter contests to do so. So I don't see that strategy changing either.

FINAL THOUGHTS

If you are a struggling Facebook advertiser in the e-commerce space, don't give up on it. It does work; you just have to figure it out. Once you find the right formula – maybe by applying some of the ideas in the book and from this interview – you'll see that there's a lot of potential and a lot of sales and revenue to be had from Facebook advertising.

If you're a seasoned, experienced company that still hasn't unlocked the potential and the impact that Facebook advertising can have on your business, you're in the same boat as well. If you've been spending money on Facebook advertising, but have found scaling to be a challenge, there are several different strategies and methodologies you can implement to start to scale your Facebook advertising successfully. Feel free to reach out to us – we'll be more than happy to help you get the results you always wanted out of Facebook.

And in general, for everyone reading this book, I hope you get tons of value out of it! This book has been a labor of love (and also of a lot of effort, energy, blood, sweat, and tears!). My goal is to deliver lots of impact and value to e-commerce companies that want to get better results out of Facebook advertising, and I hope you find it helps you in your own quest to find success with your Facebook endeavors!

Do you want to see how we have a 1500+ Return on Adspend in a competitive E-Commerce market? You can learn how to get back $15 for every $1 spend on Facebook Ads by going to www.cvoaccel.com/success.

THE GOOD STUFF

The Top Tips, Strategies, and Tactics Featured in the Book

In this chapter, you'll be able to review a summary of all the best tips, strategies, tactics, and more from our book's contributors. This chapter distills the essence of why you picked up this book. Just one of the tips here could lead you to doubling your sales (or more) in a very short time. Now, if you skipped ahead to this chapter, that's perfectly fine! Just keep in mind that these are snapshots – to get the full picture behind the strategies and tactics mentioned here, read the chapter from the Specialists behind the tips that particularly appeal to you.

AMANDA BOND

» Double down on your FB Page, since you can retarget on engagement to your page, posts, etc.

» Find out what's keeping targeted customers from buying, and use that intel in your remarketing campaigns

» Increase your LTV to be able to spend more on advertising

» Show usage cases of your product in your Instagram Stories

» Create your chatbot with a focus on authentic – not robotic – communication

» Use your chatbot to answer your FAQs

- » If you are using Webinars to sell products, split test a webinar vs. a FB Live video, track everything, and you may see a reduction in cost per attendee like Amanda did. In her split test, she saw a 500% - 700% decrease in the cost of getting a customer to attend when using FB Live video

- » Live video is 6 times more engaging than recorded video, according to stats recently released by Facebook

- » Diversify your traffic so that FB Ads isn't your only source of traffic

- » As you scale up to 7-8 figures in sales, tracking everything using UTM links is key

- » To reduce CPAs, use branding touch points (brand story videos, for example) as a first step in your Facebook Ads

- » When it comes to budgeting for your Facebook ads, decide if you want to spend money or spend time. The more money you spend up front, the faster the data comes in, and the faster you can see results. If you choose to take your time, you have to factor in all the costs associated with that, including employee time, opportunity cost, and more.

- » Stop funnel-hacking competitors; work on your own funnel instead

- » Focus on dynamic retargeting instead of ads that target cold audiences with a lead magnet or paid offer.

DAVID SCHLOSS

- » Dating-type services can advertise on Facebook now, as long as they can show that they provide a real service and are not just "scamming"

- » ICOs, cryptocurrencies, etc. cannot advertise on FB

- » Facebook massively bans advertisers while raising CPMs, CPCs, etc. once or twice a year. Don't freak out when it happens.

- » Brand story and positioning are very important elements of a FB advertising strategy

- » Videos that show products in use are more impactful than still images

- » Build a runway leading up to a launch date

- Example: Talk about the design, vision, etc. of a product or product line in video stories leading up to the day of the launch

» On a product's launch, do a live stream to generate sales and build excitement

» Use chatbots as an additional support system for customers

» Don't treat chatbots like email blasts

» Use chatbots to survey an audience before you launch a new offer, to get valuable market research data

» Use chatbots to pre-frame and pre-qualify the sales process to provide leads that are more primed to convert to your sales team

» Facebook ad costs are going up, but if you are committed and continue to test, you can optimize costs to keep them comparatively affordable for each click, lead, and customer

» Keep an eye out for mid-roll ads in the middle of Facebook video content (commercials that take place during videos), specifically in Facebook Watch episodic series

» Keep an eye on virtual reality to be able to take advantage of it when Facebook incorporates it into the platform in the future

» You can integrate your Shopify store, Amazon listings, Etsy, and more into your Facebook business page tabs

» Use an unboxing video to show the product, generate interest, and convert sales

» Use a decreasing discount offer to drive people back to your product, to buy it for the advertised discount
  - Days 1-3 - 15% discount advertised
  - Days 4-6 - 10% discount advertised
  - Days 7-9 - 5% discount advertised

» Facebook is a "pay-to-play" platform. Pay to promote your FB Page posts to get attention and views.

» Batch out 1-2 minute content videos, and have a few months' worth of content prepped and ready to go in advance

» For your Awareness content video, retarget people who have consumed 75% with a special offer saying, "We've noticed you've been watching our shows. As a token of our appreciation, we want to give you first dibs on getting 25% off the best-selling product of your choice." You get additional sales, and they get a bonus for their patronage.

» Keep promoting your content until people have consumed at least 75% of one of your videos, at which point they go into your retargeting audience and into your offer.

ENRICO LUGNAN

» Always run an engagement campaign that has nothing to do with sales whatsoever to maintain a relationship with your market

» Specific strategy:

- Grow an Instagram account to 10K+ followers

    - Note what messages, images, etc. worked best, based on engagement metrics to re-use these creatives in future ads

- Send your top 4-5 products to targeted, real, niche-specific Instagram influencers, and ask for videos or photos of them using the product in exchange. Don't come across like an "agency;" communicate with them in a casual, friendly way.

- Use the videos from influencers in a carousel ad and direct it to a cold audience, aligned with relevant interest and targeting (for Enrico's company, this consistently produced a 900%+ ROI)

» Send your product(s) to 20 to 50 influencers to get their feedback, reviews, and some free content

- This can result in influencers tagging you more than once

- If an influencer likes your product, send them a 50% off coupon to buy again and a 10% off coupon code to give to their followers to generate traffic, leads, and sales

» Use Social Blade to track growth on Instagram, YouTube, Twitch, and Twitter

- » Identify the top 5-15 questions you get asked about your product so you can automate the answering of these inquiries with a well-thought-out chatbot conversation sequence
  - Chatbots can respond to potential customers faster, in most cases, than a business or live human can
- » Focus on getting a deep understanding of your customer, which will improve everything in your marketing
  - Identify who is REALLY buying your product (example: men buying lingerie for their wives/girlfriends are an unexpected – but lucrative – target audience for lingerie companies)
- » When using Facebook Advertising, set up your funnel like so:
  - Start with content that engages with an audience
  - Retarget based on the amount of engagement
  - Create a lookalike audience based on the people who have engaged
  - Drive step-by-step custom conversions based on your unique funnel results
- » Ad spend was about the same for print ads and online ads last year (approximately$20 billion each)

JANEK MEHTA

- » Dynamic Product Ads can potentially lead to 40x ROI
- » It's a good idea to start using chatbots now, a) while they're relatively new and hot, and b) before marketers eventually ruin them
- » Leadza has been a game-changer. This software automatically goes through your Facebook Ads reporting, and texts you optimization tips (complete with specific actionable steps you can take to get better results).
- » When using video for awareness content as the first step of your Facebook ad campaigns, optimize for video views to build your audience at the lowest possible CPM, and then retarget based on the amount of consumption.

» Make sure to get the contact information for anyone who engages with your Facebook or Facebook Messenger chatbots, and incorporate them into your email list so that you – not Facebook – own the lead

» If relevant to your product, use a chatbot to capture prospects' birthdays so that you can broadcast special birthday offers to anyone whose birthday falls within the next 7 days

» Know your numbers for cold and warm traffic in your Marketing Funnel so you can use Facebook Ads effectively:

  • Cost Per Acquisition, Cost Per Lead, etc. for cold audiences and warm audiences

  • Have goals for these metrics in each stage of your funnel (example: opt-in, Add to Cart, purchase, etc.)

» The stages of a typical E-Commerce funnel are:

  • Sign up on a landing page for a free offer

  • Visit a product or sales page

  • Add to Cart

  • Initiate Checkout

  • Purchase

  • 2nd Purchase using DPAs

  • 3rd Purchase using DPAs

» A typical budget for e-comm companies is 70% allocated for cold audience campaigns and 30% for retargeting campaigns, specifically:

  • Approximately 50% for the top of the funnel

  • Approximately 30% for the middle

  • Approximately 20% for the bottom

» Maximum allowable cost per acquisition (CPA) should be your lead metric when managing and optimizing Facebook Ads

» Diversify your traffic. Don't start depending exclusively on Facebook Ads as your sole source of traffic.

» Constantly scale your brand awareness ad campaigns, not just your sale conversion campaigns, to bring more qualified traffic to your funnel

» Use Companion Labs to automate aspects of the manual bidding process to scale your best-performing ad campaigns

JEREMY HOWIE

» The 3 generally best-performing placements right now on Facebook are:
  • Video Ads
  • FB Live
  • FB Messenger Ads
» Dedicate a portion of your profits towards a non-profit that you believe in, and communicate that in your brand messaging, giving customers the opportunity to be part of something bigger
» Don't use share-bait, which asks your viewers to share or tag your ad
» Don't give out coupon codes via Messenger because it's against Facebook policy
» Use FB Messenger primarily for content delivery
  • Example: blog posts, FB Live video, etc.
» Lookalike targeting is going to overtake interest-based targeting more and more frequently in the foreseeable future
» By using and creating a lookalike audience off a customer list of even as few as 1,000 people, you can achieve very high relevance scores
» Optimize all your Facebook content for Mobile to achieve better reach, better user experience, and lower costs per impression
» Use Mobile on the top of your funnel for the cheapest impressions and acquisition costs into your funnel, then retarget on all platforms
» Create lookalike audiences based on video views for an effective cold audience that will outperform an interest-based cold audience
» Focus on user experience value of your Facebook content to get the best performance out of your ads while also aligning with Facebook's preferences

JEREMY WAINWRIGHT

» Facebook advertising is now following a relationship model, which they recommend in their advertising practice

» Little things stand out in markets and create long-term, profitable relationships with customers:

- Personalized letters
- Spending lots of time on FB Live to answer questions
- Creating thoughtful, well-planned chatbot sequences

» If you are trying to create a lifestyle business that you can step away from, make sure that you have strong systems and great people in place to run the business when you're not there

» People will tell you what they want you to say in your marketing, if you ask them.

- Survey
- Call your customers
- Get a list of most frequently asked questions from Customer Service emails, chats, etc.

» Focus on getting your Facebook Ad campaigns right before diversifying and expanding to other platforms

» Create ad images and videos that have the look of authentic content pieces, as though they were photos and videos taken by friends or family and posted in the News Feed

» Don't use discounts to get people to buy your product; use discounts to entice potential customer back to complete a purchase.

» Don't just focus on the first sale; focus on customers' lifetime value.

» The fastest-growing demographic on Facebook is the 65+ age group (who also typically have the largest amount of disposable income)

» Create lookalike audiences whenever possible. Lookalike audiences can be based on:

- People who have purchased once
- People who have purchased 3 times

- People who have purchased your upsell
- People who signed up for your email list

» Don't be afraid to run an ad to a large, broad audience, even upwards of 10 million people
  - Start when you have about 10K customers, and scale up by creating lookalike audiences

» Figure out your Customer Lifetime Value, so you know how much you can really afford to spend to acquire a customer throughout your ad campaigns

» Cold audience customer acquisition costs will be higher than warm audiences. Gauge ROI based on your combined ad campaign performance.

MARI CONNOR

» Write down the top 10 questions or objections you've heard in the last 6 months in your business, and create a Facebook post for each of them

» The top 3 profitable custom audiences are
  - Website visitors (which is why blogging and improving organic traffic is so impactful)
  - Video views
  - Email list

» Don't overuse capitals, symbols, or emojis in your ad creatives. Write ads as if they were regular messages to or from friends and family in your own Facebook feed.

» For lead generation, long-term value has been shown to be higher when you send someone to a landing page vs. having them become a lead from a lead ad

» Higher quality traffic and leads typically come from blog post visitors

» Write copy and create content as if you are really talking to someone; don't blatantly *sell* in your ads

» 5 key audiences that 90%+ of customers come from are:

- Website visitors (blog, etc.)
- Video views
- Email list
- FB page engagement
- FB likes

MIKE PISCIOTTA

» Facebook Messenger has up to 98% open rates and 50-70% click-through rates at the moment

» Once you've reached over a million people with your ads, audience overlap becomes a real issue. In order to get around this challenge, you need to create some unique configurations in your Facebook Ads setup.

» Facebook's new split testing feature leverages the power of the algorithm, and is immensely helpful when you create the unique configuration needed to resolve the audience overlap problem

» Facebook's improvements in recent years have allowed advertisers to get great performance from using "All Placements," the default setting when publishing a new ad set in a campaign. The reason: Facebook can now really pinpoint where a prospective customer is likely to convert or click.

» Facebook has been adding more placements since the News Feed has become so crowded (and, therefore, ad buying on it has become so competitive). The latest potential placement that Facebook has beta tested is Facebook Groups. The beta tests have been successful, and it's likely that they will start allowing ad placement in Groups in the near future.

» If you are new to e-commerce, do ad optimization on remarketing Add to Cart campaigns and Page Views to start
  - This will "season" your pixel with customer data, strengthening your pixel's ability to find the best people to show your ads to

» Start out by optimizing a bit further down the funnel in order to reduce initial ad costs

» Get REALLY specific in your remarketing ads, based on the product that the prospect just visited and almost checked out with

- » It can take 7-10 touches to convert a sale. So, to get the algorithm to show more impressions to the same person, use dynamic creative options (which includes randomly mixing up images and videos in an ad). This shows more variations of your ad to the same people, so you can hit a high frequency per person more consistently.

- » Empower the algorithm as much as possible, rather than controlling parameters yourself, when deploying new ad campaigns

- » If you have fewer than 5,000 customers, let the algorithm take control of the details– don't micro-manage. If you have over 5,000 customers, you can take a little more control, but even then, the algorithm should still be doing the bulk of the work.

- » With chatbots, you can only broadcast promotional material within the last 24 hours of when someone has interacted with your page, so don't blast your FB Messenger subscribers.

- » Use Slideshow ads with 5-10 product images, then retarget video views from these ads
  - • Facebook loves these ads and reduces CPM for advertisers who use them
  - • You can build a video view list
  - • You can create a lookalike from the video view list

- » When using FB Messenger ads to drive a message to leads, just give them the content right then and there in FB Messenger so they can engage with it immediately. For example, if you're offering a book, maybe give them the first chapter right in their Messenger.

- » Produce quality, focused content that your audience will love in order to attract people to your brand

MOLLY PITTMAN

- » Every brand need a story (Donald Miller's Storybrand is highly recommended)

- » Don't neglect your email list, they are your best people to monetize

- » Get into the minds of your prospects and think about what steps they take on their way to becoming buyers. Use these takeaways in your marketing.

- » It may take months of "touching" to convert a prospect to a customer. Be committed to the process.
- » People aren't buying a product, they're buying an end result
- » If you're using FB Messenger and chatbots in your ads, set the expectation that that is where the ad will go and/or how the offer will be delivered
- » Use ManyChat to sell in your chatbot sequence
- » Across various industries, lead magnet conversion rates are going down because people are sick of filling out forms online. FB Messenger and chatbots provide a seamless experience to fulfilling an offer.
- » Use FB Messenger integration with Shopify to send cart abandonment sequences via FB Messenger when someone leaves your store after getting close to checking out
- » You can use chatbot (especially if you use ManyChat) for:
  - Delivering a quote automatically
  - Delivering dynamic coupon codes
  - A lead generation "wheel of fortune" offer
- » Start building your Messenger subscribers now. Otherwise, it'll be like wishing today that you'd built a blog 10 years ago… you don't want to feel that way about Messenger 10 years from now.

SAM BELL

- » Google Display is a direct response ad placement
- » Lead with content to engage, then use smart retargeting to retarget into your offers
- » Use video for both Facebook video ads and YouTube in-stream ads
- » Research what products are in demand in your niche. Be strategic when choosing the products you'll sell. Some of your best market research sources include:
  - Amazon bestsellers

- eBay
- TV commercials
- Infomercials

» Use chatbots with their 90%+ open rates to engage your audience

» Sell products that are specific to what your audience wants; create an in-store buying experience with your bots for higher conversion rates

» Facebook News Feed ads are getting overcrowded, which is reflected in their steadily rising CPMs

» If you have an offline component to your business, use Messenger Ads to start a conversation when someone is close to your store

» If people visit your website or sales page but don't end up making a purchase, show them an ad 3 days later and invite them to ask you any questions they have that might have prevented them from purchasing. This can be done entirely via FB Messenger.

» Don't just try to sell in your chatbot; take the time to create compelling conversational sequences, which typically have a greater degree of success than attempting to use a chatbot for direct sales

» Segment your chatbot subscriber audience based on actions or inactions so you can broadcast more effectively

» Segment your visitor traffic by 7, 15, and 30 days so you can show ads that are more enticing to each group, convincing them to come back to the website or sales page

» Start testing Whatsapp-FB Ads that trigger conversions from ad to WhatsApp, in your business. There are 1 billion daily active users on WhatsApp.

» Don't discount Audience Network; use it to build up audiences for retargeting

- Target cold audiences with this ad placement to build warm audiences for ads with offers
  - Show News Feed ads
  - Show right-hand column ads

» Use custom event conversions instead of URL-set custom conversions

- » Create lookalike audiences off of your event conversion-based audiences (Add to Cart, InitiateCheckout, etc.)
- » Wicked Reports is stellar for e-comm because it pulls sales directly from the contact record, not Facebook
- » Use incentives to get multi-channel marketing information from prospects
  - Example: Specific discount or bonus if they sign up for text messages
- » Don't discount using lead ads in your e-comm marketing
- » SMS text message marketing is equivalent to FB Messenger, with similar open and click-through rates

TREVOR CHAPMAN

- » There is a myth that ugly pages convert better than "pretty" pages. In actuality, the reason ugly pages seem to convert better is that they're usually simpler than the pretty pages, and as such, don't take as long to load. Load time is the big factor here – site visitors typically do NOT wait if a page takes longer than a fraction of a second to load.
- » Think about the buyers and their process. For example, did they visit all the pages except the pricing page? If so, then pricing isn't a concern for them. Did they only visit the pricing page? Then that's their primary (or only) concern.
- » Generating ROI from advertising and competing with big companies simply comes down to creating an eloquent message that resonates with the audience
- » Focus on curing the symptom instead of just treating it. In other words, dig deep to find out why something isn't converting, rather than fixating on minutia like, say, the color of a button, and assuming that's the cause.
- » Critique your ad copy by asking yourself if you were presented with your own ad, would it convince you to buy the product?
- » There are no "participation trophies" in business. If you want to win, you have to get good at what you do.
- » You have to be able to adapt in order to stay in the game

» Put out as much content as you can (video, long post, blog, etc.) and use analytics to identify which message resonates the most. Then mine that vein until it runs dry.

» Spend your time on things that matter. Figure out the ROI of every action, task, idea, etc. before committing yourself to spending your time on it.

» Sell "necessity" items, not "accessory" ones

» Use Facebook for lead acquisition, so you can use its powerful algorithm to generate data about your prospects and buyers

  • Use other platforms for other steps in your marketing process

» In order to have enough material to upload fresh content every day, take a 3-day period once every 3 months to create all the content you'll need for that timeframe

  • Visit your competitors' sites and/or sites like BuzzSumo, and put together a list of 100 trending topics that inspire you

  • Spend those 3 days creating short videos of you talking about each topic. Create a long-form and short-form video of each, and get each video transcribed.

  • Turn your videos into:

    • Long-form and short-form videos to be posted on multiple channels (Facebook, YouTube)

    • Written posts of varying lengths (full transcripts, various edited versions, pull quotes, etc.) for multiple channels (blogs, social, etc.)

  • Post 1 piece of content to one channel or another every day (preferably multiple times per day). Make sure to mix-and-match your content – you want the video you post on YouTube, the long-form blog post, and the short-form social media post that you post on a given day to all come from different videos

» When deciding whether to boost a post, set a benchmark for yourself:

  • Trevor uses 25 shares per 10,000 views as his benchmark

  • When a post achieves or exceeds this ratio, it has resonated with your audience, and will therefore generate sales for you. You want a post like this to go viral, so keep spending money to boost it until it does.

» Don't forget to target auxiliary audiences on platforms your primary audience may not frequent. For example, if you sell camping equipment to a mostly male audience, don't forget to also target their gift-giving significant others on Pinterest or Facebook with something like a "Top 10 Gifts for Men Who Love the Great Outdoors" post

» With marketing, tactics may change, but underlying principles are always the same

RORY STERN

» Remove your emotions from the results in your business

» Keep up-to-date on Facebook Ads policy

» The Facebook Ad platform frowns on advertisers who create an exclusively "buy, buy, buy"-type experience

» Don't crowdsource your Facebook Ads advice. Find a mentor, a system, or a training program to follow from start to finish.

» Facebook doesn't teach you to be a direct response marketer, it teaches you to be a brand advertiser

» Think about what people *don't* like when you are brainstorming your targeting

» Think about your advertising as a long-term investment in your company or brand, not a short-term solution to make a quick buck. Don't expect to make millions instantly on Facebook.

» Break down your Facebook Ads data into custom conversions to identify where and what to optimize in your marketing funnel process (Example: If Add to Cart is the big drop off, optimize your website or checkout process)

» Lead generation is your gold mine. You should be constantly generating leads, finding people who are interested in your product.

» In E-Commerce, it's not just about sending people to your store. Focus on the back-end (customer relationships, offering more products, bundles, subscriptions, etc.), where the real money is.

- Don't be afraid to acquire customers at break-even, or even at a loss! Focus on the back-end, and you can quickly monetize your customers beyond the initial cost of advertising to acquire them.

» Think about something that you can give away for free that is a) super cheap for you to acquire, and b) related to your product/niche/etc.

» Don't sell crappy products

» Pay attention to your FB Page comments, since they can potentially affect future ad costs.

- Plus, it's a good opportunity to contact customers and resolve their issues

» If you have a Shopify store, use the built-in features that work with FB Messenger to leverage the FB Messenger channel right away

» You absolutely need to be using FB Messenger and advanced marketing automation bot software

» Make sure you lead your product or customer down a path to a good experience and/or a measurable, trackable ROI

» Use FB Messenger and chatbots to send customer-experience-enhancing videos (unboxing photo/video, video of how to set up the product, etc.)

» First-time customer coupons are basic, but work well for lead generation

» Run a giveaway contest for your product or a bundle of your products, and build an email list from the people who enter. Once the contest ends, you can target this ready-made list of people who have already demonstrated interest in your product.

» Use deep discounts to get people into your funnel and then sell, sell, sell on the back-end.

» Focus on customer support. Don't neglect it – people buy the experience as much as they do the product

JOSH MARSDEN

» Leveraging all stages in your Facebook Advertising is KEY in advertising today:

  - Awareness

  - Engagement

  - Conversion

  - Monetization

» Think of Facebook advertising as a "layered system" of Facebook Ads

» Don't run ads without proper measuring in place (Don't hope for results….)

» Don't rely on just your website for new customer acquisition; use a funnel, especially with paid advertising

» Facebook's algorithm is smart, to the point where you don't have to overthink targeting by creating a very narrow audience. The algorithm makes it possible for even bigger audiences to generate results.

» Advertising competition on Facebook is increasing, and your ability to market through the ad creative is what will separate you from your competition

» Instagram Story ads have cheap lead generation acquisition rates at the moment, because at least for the time being, competition is low on this placement

» With a low ad spend budget, follow this strategy to generate ROI:

  - Drive cold traffic to a great offer presented in a video ad

  - Retarget with brand-building, engaging content

  - Retarget that same audience with a "sweeten the deal"-type approach, where you are offering a bigger discount or a bonus. Increase that over time too with new ads.

» Use Dynamic Product Ads to target your customers and get them to return to your website to make additional purchases

» For a product validation strategy, you can use Upviral or a simple landing page that markets a contest to win your product or product bundle

Now that you've read this list of all the best tips, strategies, and tactics in this book, take a deeper look at the one(s) that resonated most powerfully with you, that feel(s) most relevant to your business. Who came up with them? Now, go back to that specialist's chapter, so you can read about it in more depth (along with many other potentially useful suggestions) directly from the specialist him/herself!

When you are applying the tip, strategy, or tactic to your business, be sure to implement it exactly as the specialist recommends, without a single missed detail. Go through this process for every tip, strategy, and tactic that you picked up from this chapter so you have all the information you need to successfully incorporate the advice into your own business.

> *Do you want to see how we have a 1500+ Return on Adspend in a competitive E-Commerce market? You can learn how to get back $15 for every $1 spend on Facebook Ads by going to **www.cvoaccel.com/success.***

CONCLUSION

This book started by describing how a few notable figures shrewdly leveraged trends, with spectacular results. After looking at the examples set by Henry Ford, Elon Musk, and the Winklevoss twins, you can see why paying attention to trends, figuring out how to adapt, and then taking action can make your company more successful. This book is designed to be a shortcut to helping you understand the trends happening in Facebook Advertising right now, and how they affect E-Commerce companies in 2019. This book is also designed to help you figure out how to adapt quickly, so that these trends neither hurt your business, nor become missed opportunities for growth.

The only thing this book can't do is actually make the necessary changes for you. After reading it, you've learned what the trends are and how to adapt – now it's up to you to take action! This means that you may need to:

- Work on your mindset as a Facebook Advertiser, based on the collective teachings of the advertisers in this book, so you approach Facebook Advertising the right way"
- Review your Facebook Ad usage to determine which ad campaigns should be cut, based on the trends shared here as well as any rising costs that you've observed in your specific ad campaigns
- Make sure that your Facebook Advertising account is set up with the pixel, custom conversions, events, and reporting – 100% set up

and running without any problems so you can measure like a true direct-response marketer

- Identify opportunities in your Facebook Ads account for new ad campaigns that allow you to implement the strategies shared in this book
- Roll out and measure new Facebook Ad campaigns to test some of the strategies shared in this book
- Generate new ad creatives to leverage placements, like Instagram Story ads, so you can improve placement performance

The bottom line here is that the advertising businesses that rise to the top, the ones that produce massive ROI from Facebook Ads, are those that don't just consume content, but take massive action. Whether you take your cues directly from the book, or extrapolate another strategy on your own, my advice to you is to take action right away – as soon as you close this book! You can do it yourself, delegate to a team member, or hire outside help that knows what they are doing (hint, hint).

Either way, no matter what your situation, be sure to take advantage of all the value offered to you with this book:

STEP 1

Go to **www.cvoaccel.com/fbbonus** to download a free gift, just for picking up this book. This free gift includes:

» **The Perfect Facebook Advertising Plan for E-Com** - An easy to follow, step-by-step, strategy plan, which explains how to build a full-featured Facebook Advertising funnel with cold, warm, and hot traffic, retargeting stacks, and more!

» **Facebook Advertising Success Kit** - This kit includes Reporting templates that you can use to track ad performance, set your performance goals, and compare your performance against averages today!

» **Free 7 Day Trial to the E-Commerce Success Summit All Access Pass** - This includes over 50 interviews with some of the top names in entrepreneurship and digital marketing today, including Scott Oldford, Dennis Yu, Matt Clark, Todd Brown, and many more!

STEP 2

Join our free E-Commerce Success Group at
**www.facebook.com/groups/
ecomsuccessgroup**

» In our **E-Commerce Success Group**, you'll be able to interact with other E-Commerce business owners who are actively hustling to increase their success in E-Commerce, just like you! You will also have access to me and several of my friends in the entrepreneur space, who can help you in your business.

Now, if you are ready to accelerate your success by hiring a coach or a team to implement the strategies in this book, you can reach out to my company and me directly at **www.cvoaccel.com/win** to apply to receive a 100% free complimentary consultation.

FINAL WORDS

At the end of the day, it's up to you to create the E-Commerce business you want. Facebook does not dictate your success or failure – you do! That's the beauty of owning your own business – you are in the driver's seat. Practice gratitude, trust yourself, work hard, listen to mentors, be coachable, and take constant, massive action.

With this approach, especially if you follow this book and take advantage of the shortcut that it represents, you will see major results. We live in a very exciting moment in time, one where you have the potential to create a massively successful E-Commerce business that can produce several lifetimes' worth of wealth. This can set up your retirement, your kids' future, your kids' kids' future, and more. Every step that you take, win or lose, is progress.

Yes, even losing is progress because failure is the greatest teacher. Keep this in mind when business gets tough, you get stressed, and you're tempted to throw in the towel. Play the mental game well – always keep your head in the game by staying positive, optimistic, and appreciative of every difficult moment, because each one is a lesson that gets you one step closer to your ultimate goal.

The world is truly your oyster, and your E-Commerce company is your ship to the world that you want to live in. Sail it with poise, positive thinking, hard work, and an open mind, and eventually, you will reach your personal Utopia.

ACKNOWLEDGEMENTS

When I committed to publishing a book on Facebook Ads to serve E-Commerce business owners, I had very little idea what I was getting into…

Publishing a book takes about a hundred steps, perseverance, and hard work.

Luckily, I have many people to thank for helping me get this book out to you to help you with your E-Commerce Business.

To start, the amazing entrepreneurs that have contributed to this book were incredible in their contributions. I'm truly honored to be your peer. Special thanks goes to J. Trevor Chapman, Molly Pittman, Mike Pisciotta, Jeremy Howie, Enrico Lugnan, Janak Mehta, Rory Stern, Sam Bell, David Schloss, Mari Connor, Amanda Bond, and Jeremy Wainwright for contributing amazing content to this book.

I also want to thank the team at Writers Cartel with Aaron Wang and Tatiana Hutton for bringing this book to life and pulling me to the finish line on it because of my crazy schedule.

The book cover was designed by the top-notch team at Studio 1 Design, led by Design Guru, Greg Merrilees. There's a reason why the best of the best in the internet marketing world use his team

Kelly Exeter, thank you for coming in, sorting the book's interior design, and running this to the end zone. Hey, what can I say… I grew up in Texas where football is treated ceremoniously like a religion.

Finally, thank you Adam Lyons for the conversation that spawned this idea. You have been an incredible friend and I appreciate you.

I have so many friends that I'm grateful for so if I miss someone, my apologies. The journey of entrepreneurship and growing a business is the biggest mountain that I've ever hiked on and will probably ever hike on. Without many of you, it would have been a much less enjoyable and successful journey.

In no particular order, thank you for helping and supporting me on my Entrepreneur Journey...

Rich Thurman, Devolis Newburn, Rodney Hearns, Scott Oldford, Ryan Deiss, Richard Lindner, Kendra Wright, Joanna Ulloa, Justin Walsh, Jennifer Kem, Ben Thompson, Tahnee Lynch, Daniel Joseph, Ian Erlandson, Dirk Littrell, Kelsey Bratcher, Dustin Young, Josh Stockton, Greg Hickman, Adam Sell, Tim Falcone, Valerie Falcone, John Mikan, David Gonzalez, Gonzalo Paternoster, Ryan McKenzie, Shannon Hernandez, Josh Stepenenko, Curt Maly, Andrew O'Brien, Sean Whalen, Joe Polish, Earnest Epps, Shawn Byrnes, Rudi Ornelas, Jason Valasek, Joshua Valentine, Nicholas Bayerle, Kathy Buchanan Yturralde, Mike Gelblicht, Karl Schuckert, Todd Brown, Kevin Donahue, JimmyTay Trinh, Nick Cirello, Aurelijus Terminas, Trish Sanderson, Nicholay Okorokov, Kamila Zamaro, Vikki Mattera, Marisa Tusha, Jek Tibayan, Nick Silikov, Markus Heitkoetter, Pat Johnson, Dave Albano, Ross Walker, Damian Rufus, Raven Kleinbach, Daryl Hill, Jaime Masters, Daniela Moreno, Jesus Diaz, Leticia Diaz, Dornubari Pope Vizor, David Nguyen, Kraig Kubicek, Jeremy Montoya, Vin Featherstone, Jonathan Khorsandi, Kathy Goughenour, Tony Martin, Dan Martell, Michael Lovitch, Hollis Carter, Joshua B Lee, John Lee Dumas, Freddy Lansky, Michael Keefrider, Kate Erickson, Navid Moazzez, Jamal Miller, Kevin Breeding, James Schramko, John Dennis, Esther Kiss, Jon Schumacher, Arjun Brara, Heather Ann Havenwood, Katya Sarmiento, Brian Bargiel, Russell Lundstrom, Kristina Rueling, Jesse Elder, Jon Morrow, Ron Reich, Charl Coetzee, Phil Randazzo, Greg Reid, Dennis Yu, Brian Kurtz, Diana Lane, Brandon Campbell, Lain Ehmann, Wes Schaeffer, Ted Miller III, Guillaume Couillard, Chris Mercer, Valerie Viramontes, Grant Andrew, Adan Perez, Sarah Laws, Jay Patel, Ian Garlic, Jay Fiset, Ivan Glushko, Uli Iserloh, Caitlin Pyle, Brian Johnson, Jeff Nabers, Rachel Nabers, Victoriya Scovel, Tony Tovar, Austin Iuliano, Chad Collins, Justin Christianson, Daniel Rose,

Chris Lee, John Davy, Allen Brouwer IV, David Rice, Troy Salewske, George Macrodimitris, Henry Gridley, Aaron Wiseman, Adrian James, Richard Cussons, David Littrell, Luke Pawlikow, Alexander Willoughby, Kara Pierce, Scott Desgrosseilliers, Chandler Bolt, Ryan Levesque, Rachel Wilmann, Craig Dewe, Jovan Will, Fernando Godinez, Richard Miller, Chen Yen, Andy Hussong, Pat Flynn, Graham English, Tony Alfreda, Kimberly Bean Holmes, Rob Holmes, Jon Marino, Zach Johnson, Ian Stanley, Peter Bragino, Guido Bonelli, Janet Beckers, Rob Hegarty, Phly Jambor, Michell Corr, Ed Wotring, Justin Rondeau, Christian Burris, Ian Nagy, Chase Frost, Chip Baker, Michael Hunter, Jacki Mclenaghan, Lisa Schulteis, Melodie Moore, Carrie Lynn-Rodenberg, Deborah Hanchey, Scott Wells, Piyush Parikh, Kevin Mogavero, Ed O'Keefe, Roland Frasier, Tommie Powers, Dobbin Buck, Cory Snyder, Justin Sandy, Mikal Abdullah, Jess Wilkinson, Josh Wilkinson, Zach Obront, Jayson Gaignard, Debra Stangl, Rachel Kersten, Greig Wells, Lynika Cruz, Chuck Trautman, Kim Snider, Charlie Lyons, Monaica Ledell, Lea Rosa Garcia, Christian Bonilla, Kevin Johnson, Patrick Phenix, Dominick Sirianni, Meghan Alonso, Marc Mawhinney, Niel Issa, Janet Issa, Bret Thomson, Garrett Cannon, Sophia Bera, David Bullock, Nikki Black, Chris Higbee, John Howell, Wardee Harmon, Robert Michon, Michael Anthony, Angela Kerr, Gene Morris, Andrea Hale, Joel Young, Andrew Warner, Ethan Sigmon, Kim Phillips, Josh Turner, Chris Danilo, Nick Jensen, Adam Teece, Lawton Chiles, Regina Bellows, Russ Henneberry, Nolan Nissle, Kathy Lane, Burhaan Pattel, Mark Bailey, Michael Mathewson, Ryan Farrell, Chris Copp, Jet Berelson, Tamsin Silver, Chris Plough, Peter Li, Carlos Alvarez, Jeanna Pool, Roger Miller, Katie Miller, Shane Smith, Jenny Holla, Robyn Jackson, Tyler Bramlett, Jennifer Patterson, Tracy Matthews, Lindsey Yturralde, Alecia Smith, Scott Vogel, Matt Esaena, Scott Voelker, Tabitha Armstrong, Lisa Kuecker, Erika Rodriguez, Candy Rodriguez, Becky De Acetis, Phil Costantino, Jake Spear, Kimberly Najarro, Ricky Baldasso, Ben Cummings, John Allen Mollenhauer, Nicole Munoz, Ron White, Michelle McGlade, James Roper, Colin Morgan, John Belcher, Justin Brooke, Geeta Sidhu-Robb, and, last but not least, the Digital Marketer, Infusionsoft, Superfast Business, and Baby Bathwater teams and communities.

Most importantly, I want to thank my family, Mom, Dad, Bob, Rachel, Laney, Cody, Roscoe, Kolby, and my son. My family has always stood by me through the toughest moments of my life to date. I love you guys with all my heart. To my son, without you, I not only wouldn't have become an Entreprenuer and now an Author, but I would have never became the man that I am today. Thank you for coming into my life and being my "shining light."

STAY IN TOUCH

If you have any thoughts or comments you'd like to share with me about the book, please email me at josh@cvoaccel.com.

I would also recommend that you head on over to www.cvoacceleration. com and subscribe to our list to receive more valuable content, similar to this book, delivered weekly.

You can also follow me on:

- **Facebook:** facebook.com/cvoacceleration
- **Twitter:** @cvoacceleration
- **Instagram:** @joshuaamarsden
- **LinkedIn:** linkedin.com/in/joshmarsden

If you appreciated the value and hard work that went into this book, I would love it if you were to tag me on Instagram with a photo of you holding this book. That would really make my day.

Keep in touch!

Josh Marsden, MBA

Made in the USA
Lexington, KY
27 July 2019